U.S. Corporate Profitability and Capital Formation

(Pergamon Policy Studies—47)

Pergamon Policy Studies on U.S. and International Business

PERGAMON POLICY STUDIES

ON U.S. AND INTERNATIONAL BUSINESS

U.S. Corporate Profitability and Capital Formation

Are Rates of Return Sufficient?

Herman I. Liebling

Pergamon Press

NEW YORK • OXFORD • TORONTO • SYDNEY • FRANKFURT • PARIS

Pergamon Press Offices:

U.S.A. Pergamon Press Inc., Maxwell House, Fairview Park, Elmsford, New York 10523, U.S.A.

U.K. Pergamon Press Ltd., Headington Hill Hall, Oxford OX3 0BW, England

CANADA Pergamon of Canada, Ltd., 150 Consumers Road, Willowdale, Ontario M2J, 1P9, Canada

AUSTRALIA Pergamon Press (Aust) Pty. Ltd., P O Box 544, Potts Point, NSW 2011, Australia

FRANCE Pergamon Press SARL, 24 rue des Ecoles, 75240 Paris, Cedex 05, France

FEDERAL REPUBLIC OF GERMANY Pergamon Press GmbH, 6242 Kronberg/Taunus, Pferdstrasse 1, Federal Republic of Germany

Library of Congress Cataloging in Publication Data

Liebling, Herman I
  U.S. corporate profitability and capital
formation.

  (Pergamon policy studies)
  Bibliography: p.
  Includes index.
  1. Corporate profits—United States.
2. Saving and investment—United States.
I. Title.
HC110.P7L53 1979   338.5'16'0973   79-14095
ISBN 0-08-024622-2

Printed in the United States of America

Contents

List of Figures and Tables

Preface

While profit trends of an individual company typically command the interest of investors year in and year out, its performance as part of macroeconomic policy appears to be of intermittent interest. Rightfully, however, the rate of return on investment, should it have declined in recent years as this study shows, surely has contributed to the decline in the growth of capital formation and productivity that has characterized the U.S. economy since 1973. In the nonfarm business economy, the decline in productivity growth from 2.0 percent per year in 1965-73 to 0.8 percent in 1973-78 and 0.5 percent in 1978 raises serious difficulties affecting fulfillment of this nation's responsibilities. Primary among these are the U.S. capabilities to deal with our domestic and international obligations towards raising living standards of peoples, both here and abroad. Moreover, the decline in productivity growth represents a crucial setback in limiting the accelerated pace of inflation in recent years, perhaps the major social disturbance of the present age. The cushioning effect that productivity exerts in reducing wage and other cost pressures on prices is lost in this process. Finally, as investment and productivity lag, barriers to inflation diminish even in periods of slow growth, as business costs continue to rise and "stagflation" is made increasingly possible.

Of course, no single cause explains the decline in productivity growth. The slowing may have derived from changes in the age distribution of the labor force, as less productive teenagers and women increased as a share of the total; higher costs of environmental legislation (both directly as a more expensive input, and indirectly as a deterrent to investment); substitution of more labor for energy-using capital equipment; etc.

Manifestly, however, the slow-up in growth of capital stock would appear to be an important factor in contributing to declining productivity growth. The capital-labor ratio in nonfarm industries has grown only 0.9 percent per annum since 1973, contrasting with the 2.2 percent growth between 1948 and 1973. The decline in growth of the net stock of capital is even more striking. Between 1973 and 1978, growth of production facilities (though inclusive of environmental outlays) was 2.4 percent, which compares with 4.5 percent during 1965-73 and with 3.6 percent when the entire 1948-73 period is considered.

Profitability in the U.S. economy surely is related to the investment process. While the sufficiency of demand needs to be considered before investment is encouraged, expected rates of return must be a second blade of the scissor in the investment decision. In that respect, current profitability resolves that decision, as many studies have shown. Moreover, those rates of return are reflected in stock market prices, whose performance in recent years appears lackluster at best in support of capital formation.

It is to the resolution of problems with respect to whether rates of return are sufficient to encourage investment that this book is directed. More specifically, the objectives of this study were:

- To supply an analysis for economic policymakers and the literate public which might resolve the issue of the trend in profitability over the past three decades. Though complex econometric methods of analyses were utilized, so were some relatively simple procedures that might be readily comprehensible to noneconomists. Indeed, where complexities arose, simplification in exposition was provided, sometimes with sacrifice of supporting materials not herein included. In any event, that objective of exposition and simplification might explain to economists why some topics have been addressed in what might be considered summary fashion.

- To provide a compendium of statistics bearing on profitability, which could serve as a reference data base for persons seeking information and analysis in this field. The dozens of tables which have been provided in the statistical appendix should supply much material to fact-seekers. Aside from the conclusions of the study, these tables may prove helpful in providing the statistical framework for other studies.

- To furnish a comprehensive review and analysis of the literature pertaining to the recent trend in profitability of nonfinancial corporations that provides the substance of these works in a handy and nontechnical manner.

Much more work than appears here needs to be done on trends in profitability. Accordingly, the conclusions reached herein must be considered tentative. That should not be surprising nor disappointing in view of the 200 years or so that economists and accountants have addressed themselves merely to the problem of defining profits, let alone profitability or rates of return. Hopefully, official and other sources will continue to provide funds for further research in this area.

Though the author has been concerned with trends in profitability for nearly a decade, much of the materials presented herein were developed with financial assistance provided in 1978 by the Office of the Secretary, United States Department of the Treasury.

Acknowledgments

The merits that may be found in this study resulted from the combined efforts of a team. Throughout, Mr. Robert Ott managed required computer program services, organized the tables, and contributed to the interpretation of the data. Mr. Lawrence Summers provided an early draft of the review of the relevant literature. Ms. Joy C. Olgyay helped in computer assistance and advice at a preliminary stage of the study, as did Ms. Lois Fulmer during that period. Mr. David Kohls was responsible for preparing and revising final tables and charts and was generally helpful as a research assistant. Mrs. June Vail typed the final manuscript. However, all errors in the study should be attributed to the author.

Mrs. Beatrice Vaccara, Deputy Assistant Secretary of the United States Treasury Department (Economic Policy) was extremely helpful in suggestions regarding the form in which this study appears. Of course, she, too, is blameless for errors of substance.

1 Summary and Public Policy Issues

In several widely cited studies in recent years, profitability or the rate of return on corporate capital was perceived to have declined during the 1970s to 30-year lows — but only because of special factors which already have, or soon would, wane in influence. (Cagan & Lipsey, 1978; Chimerine & Himmelstein, 1979; Feldstein & Summers, 1977). Statistically processed by so-called "cyclical adjustments," by allowances for an ascribed transient squeeze from higher costs of energy, and by other special and temporary influences, the preadjusted, measured, low profit rates recorded in the 1970s are thereby raised. (A review of the relevant literature is presented in Chapter 3.)

In their cyclically adjusted form, the rates of return appear not at all ominous, especially if pretax trends are observed. Indeed, these "adjusted" rates have been interpreted to be in the normal range; if anything, they are concluded as being precursive to an improved performance in the "measured" rates. The recent preadjusted figures for 1976 and 1977, in these studies, already are considered to have fluctuated within the normal range previously observed in the "good" years of the post-World War II period.

One consequence of this conclusion is that rates of return, especially on a pretax basis, need not generate much concern for economic policymakers. Of course, some room is left for policy change — since lowered economic growth and investment in the 1970s surely could not be ignored. This finds expression in recommendations for improved aftertax rates of return, presumably to be attained by reduction in corporate tax rates.

If this conclusion of a current satisfactory state of pretax profits were to be accepted, economic policy initially could be directed merely to the maintenance of high level economic activity. (Robust economic growth was a condition which surely prevailed in 1976 and 1977 and, accordingly, profitability in these years already was judged by some to be in the "normal" range.) High level economic activity would ensure adequate pretax rates of return, assuming that the cyclical adjustments

1

in these studies were valid. Together with adjustment in tax rates, that would be deemed sufficient to attain the higher rates of capital formation thought necessary to increase our capacity to produce, to raise living standards, and to moderate inflation.

A by-product of this view is that a boom in the stock market merely awaits more general awareness of this "normality" in profitability.

A SUMMARY STATEMENT OF THE CONCLUSION

The adequacy in pretax rates of return that has been found in these recent studies rests on uncertain ground. Though special factors did abound, the case for the special nature of the 1970s is not convincing in explaining low profitability. Not the least for such is the faulty use of dummy variables, as utilized in these econometric studies, which appeared to validate the importance of special factors that could explain why measured rates were low and why they would not permanently remain low.

Moreover, the choice of which among many plausible "rates of return" as the standard by which to view profitability is not beyond criticism – much depending on whether company-recorded or real economic profits (or inclusive or exclusive of interest paid on capital supplied through debt) was used in the numerator. Book profits, which are based on historical rather than replacement cost, remain the typical basis of corporate accounts. This results in bloating earnings; making them look unduly high and subject to public criticism; and distorting the numerator in rates of return calculations. The latter are affected also by whether total or physical capital at company-recorded or real costs was used in the denominator.

Finally, the difficulties of measuring rates of return have been especially complicated by the distortions caused by inflation, which has affected the valuation of most elements of the balance sheet and the income statement. Nevertheless, those studies which make "inflation adjustments" do not appear to have taken into account the full range of benefits and costs of inflation on corporate debt. Because of their net debtor status, inflation generates a gain to nonfinancial corporations as the real value of liabilities declines. In some studies, such gains are added to profits (Cagan and Lipsey, 1978). However, this adjustment for inflation is incomplete; no account is made of the loss to corporations in their creditor status in pension funds, whose assets decline in value with inflation and thereby raise contingent liabilities.

In contrast with those that support a view of normal or usual profitability, the overall conclusion of this study is that lowered rates of return on both pre- and posttax bases have developed in the 1970s; and, moreover, that they reflect more than transient influences. Indeed, a permanent or structural change to lowered profitability apparently was initiated as long ago as the mid-1960s.

A CAPSULE OF THE FINDINGS

As previously noted, the interpretation of trends in profit rates has always been difficult. To restate, such different measures may be utilized in the numerator as profits before tax, profits after tax, historical or replacement cost of inventory change and depreciation charges, and assigned gains to equity resulting from the reduced real value of the debt due to inflation; while the denominator might utilize net worth (with or without adjustment for updating the value of physical assets) or total assets on an historical or replacement basis. The inclusion of interest paid by corporations in the numerator also yields a somewhat different perspective to the trend in profit rates. Finally, another approach to profitability frequently used is the profit share to total value of output – which in many respects overcomes the balance sheet problems of valuation of assets and liabilities. (These issues are treated in detail in Chapter 2).

Approximate and differing in concept though they are, most standard measures of corporate profitability, nevertheless, have registered significant declines in trend since the mid-1960s.

- Favorable productivity conditions propelled rates of return upward in the mid-1960s to an historical peak in post-World War II experience. However, the sharp descent from those mid-1960 peaks toward lesser profitability in recent years has represented more than a decline from so-called over-inflated or unusual rates of the mid-1960s.

- Cyclical adjustments do not bring current profit rates back to a normal range. Indeed, this study utilized several varieties of cyclical adjustments and found lower rates of return to have developed even on the basis of the most optimistic view of potential capacity (which would have exerted the maximum lift on recorded profit rates).

- Trends toward lesser profitability in the 1970s are striking on either the pretax or the posttax corporate profits bases; and also when net interest paid by corporations is either included or excluded.

An interesting aspect of the results of this study is the apparently large decline in the 1970s in rates of return on a pretax plus interest paid basis – "capital income" (see table 1.1). As adjusted by the procedures of the official national accounts for the exclusion of inventory gains and the replacement cost of depreciation, the pretax capital income return on investment was reduced by four percentage points in the 1970s, as compared with the 1948-69 period. The decline becomes even sharper when interest paid is not included as earnings on capital. As noted earlier, the pretax rates of return for the 1970s are said in some studies to be aberrant and self-corrective in nature. This is a contention that this study disputes on the basis of econometric

Table 1.1. Rates of Return, Nonfinancial Corporations*
(percent)

| | Pretax | | Posttax | |
Period	With Interest	Without Interest	With Interest	Without Interest
1949-69	13.1	12.1	6.9	6.0
1950-59	12.7	12.1	5.8	5.3
1960-69	13.4	12.1	8.0	6.6
1970-78	9.4	7.1	5.7	3.3

*Profits before or after taxes and inclusive or exclusive of interest paid as percent of stock of reproducible physical assets at replacement cost.

experiments more elaborate than those shown in Feldstein and Summers (1977) and the Council of Economic Advisors (1978). Accepting the latter's contention, proposed reform of tax legislation – which would affect only posttax return – would represent only a partial step towards the resolution of the general problem of lowered profitability in the 1970s.

On the basis of the capital income concept, the posttax returns on investment also register declines in the 1970s, but less so than on the pretax basis. Primarily, the interest component of the capital income contributes to this result. The sharp increase in interest paid in recent years reflects heavier reliance on the debt markets to finance investment and higher interest rates. The deductibility of interest cost in contrast with dividends for tax purposes favors debt. Therefore, the posttax capital income rate of return appears less depressed, relative to equity.

Without interest paid being considered (i.e., using corporate earnings as such in the numerator), returns to corporations on a posttax basis also are seen to have declined sharply, as table 1.1 shows. Indeed, the decline in posttax profitability is particularly impressive (and ominous, from the investment incentive standpoint) in view of legislated tax reductions in recent years, whose effect was to dampen the rise in the tax "bite," but not to reverse it, as shown below. This decline in posttax profitability has reflected the growing importance of "illusory" inflation-caused book profits, which remain taxable. When adjustments are made to eliminate additions to profits which reflect merely the effects of inflation on historically costed inventories and depreciation, the effective tax rate is seen to have increased, as shown in table D3 in the Statistical Appendix.

An issue arises with respect to the significance of including or excluding interest paid, as part of the return on capital. This study would judge that, despite tax advantages, it is not conclusive that the return to capital supplied by both equity plus debt holders is always the relevant concept to observe in the framework of the factors affecting the investment decision of the corporation. Indeed, since the proportion of long-term debt to corporate capital stabilized in the 1970s, rising interest rates represent a deterrent to investment, as well as a factor contributing to lowered rates of return on equity. Consequently, corporations would tend to evaluate expected rates of return on an aftertax basis and exclusive of the interest paid component.

Though tax advantages apply to debt and "real" capital gains on debt are said by academicians to arise from inflation, interest payments nevertheless may be viewed as much a cost as any other expense. Of course, that expense would be weighed against whatever additional income is generated by obtaining debt capital. Moreover, as noted previously, corporations may be creditors in their pension funding capacity, which may well offset gains from inflation in their debtor positions. Overall, the gains from inflation to corporate debt holders, if they were to be considered real, appear to be a concept that is held more commonly in classrooms than in corporate boardrooms. (For further discussion of the social return to capital, see Chapter 2.)

THE "CYCLICALLY ADJUSTED" RESULTS

The downdrift in profitability appears in most measurements herein presented even after allowance is made for cyclical effects which might contribute only temporarily to the appearance of a decline. The downdrift is evident in the results of complex econometric experiments as well as in the simpler approaches.

One major set of statistics affirms a conclusion of a secular downdrift in profitability, even before cyclical adjustment. Using 1949-77 as the long-term average as a standard, the rate of return of pretax "capital income" on reproducible capital assets at 12 percent compares with the 1970-77 rate of 9 percent. However, since this reduced rate in the 1970s might indicate merely cyclical effects or repercussions of special circumstances, some studies have raised profitability rates by means of "cyclical adjustment." The conventional and official CEA procedure has been to raise recorded rates of return by a factor assumed to represent the closing of the gap between actual and potential gross national product (GNP), as calculated by the President's Council of Economic Advisors in 1978. Adjusting rates of return to a "full employment" basis is justified as a procedure in symmetry with the "full employment" budget concept, which is intended to eliminate the effect of cyclical swings on receipts.

This study, however, has utilized several new measurements of the "GNP gap" to make cyclical adjustments (see fig. 1.1). After application of these several alternatives of cyclical adjustment, profitability rates are observed as having drifted lower in the 1970s in all of these measures, as shown in table 1.2.

Moreover, much doubt now exists that potential GNP growth trends of the past, which are incorporated in the official GNP gap calculations used by Feldstein and Summers (1977) and by the Council of Economic Advisors (1978), can easily be regained. The recent history of revisions

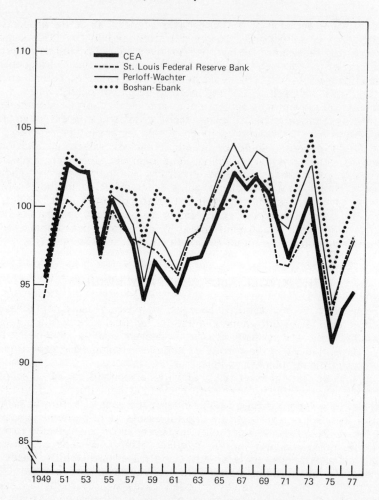

Fig. 1.1. Alternative measures of gap between
actual and potential and trend GNP.

in such measurements points to earlier overestimates of potential GNP. As productivity worsened in 1978, the likelihood increased that this pattern of reduction in estimates of growth of potential GNP will be extended. The 1979 <u>Economic Report</u> again lowered recent year estimates of potential GNP.

But even when the several official and private 1978 estimates of GNP gap were used in making cyclical adjustments, rates of profitability were not substantially raised. Indeed, one such cyclical adjustment – based on "trend" rather than "GNP gap" measurements – shows virtually no change in rates of return from the "actuals" as shown in table 1.2.

However, one defect of nearly all recent studies of profitability is the assumption that the profitability trend is discernable only under the assumption of full employment, that is to say, a closed GNP gap; or that

Table 1.2. Nonfinancial Corporations:
Rates of Return on Profits Before Tax (NIPA) Plus Interest
on Depreciable Assets, Actual and Cyclically Adjusted*
(percent)

Averages	Actual	Cyclically Adjusted By			
		CEA Gap	St. Louis "Fed" Gap	Perloff-Wachter Gap	"Trend" Gap
1949-77	12.1	12.8	13.1	11.9	11.9
1950-59	12.7	13.0	13.6	12.5	12.4
1960-69	13.4	13.9	13.5	13.1	12.9
1949-69	13.1	13.5	13.7	12.9	12.8
1970-77	9.4	11.0	11.3	10.1	9.4

---

*The cyclical adjustments are based on coefficients developed by statistical regressions of rates of return on time and the various estimates of the gap between actual and potential GNP. CEA Gap is from January 1978 Economic Report of the President. Beginning year in 1949 for St. Louis "Fed" and "Trend" Gaps; 1955 for Perloff-Wachter Gap.

the several manufacturing capacity utilization rates (which also are used in some studies for cyclical adjustments) are at boom levels. Surely, the economy has not, nor will it in the near future, perform in the fashion required to close (or overclose) the earlier official estimates of the gap; nor will it be considered desirable to return to the overheated 1973 operating rates in manufacturing, which led to inflationary pressures.

The results of procedures using the several cyclical adjustments also were made on other profitability concepts — before and after taxes and with and without interest paid. Total depreciable assets at current cost were typically used as the denominator. By and large, the deterioration in profitability in the 1970s also is evident in each such case after adjustment for cyclical influences by the several measures. (The tables on rates of return after cyclical adjustment are shown in full detail in the Statistical Appendix.)

Of special interest were the figures relating to profits after taxes, without inclusion of interest paid. As noted previously, the incentive to invest by corporations probably is highly influenced by aversion to high interest cost, the desire to avoid debt, the preference for reliance on internal funds, etc. Though debt is preferentially treated relative to equity financing under present tax law, the desirability of equity financing remains a factor in the investment decision, especially in view of the doubling of yield in high grade corporate bonds in the mid-1970s, as compared with the 1960s. Under these circumstances, a doubling of the pay-out ratio from the investment would need to be assured to retain the equivalent return of the 1960s.

Table 1.3. Nonfinancial Corporations:
Rates of Return on Profits After Tax (NIPA) on
Depreciable Assets, Actual and Cyclically Adjusted*
(percent)

Year Averages	Actual	Cyclically Adjusted By			
		CEA Gap	St. Louis "Fed" Gap	Perloff-Wachter Gap	"Trend" Gap
1949-77	5.3	5.6	5.7	5.3	5.2
1950-59	5.3	5.4	5.7	5.5	5.2
1960-69	6.6	6.8	6.7	6.4	6.3
1949-69	6.0	6.2	6.3	6.1	5.8
1970-77	3.3	4.0	4.2	3.7	3.3

*The cyclical adjustments are based on coefficients developed by statistical regressions of rates of return on time and the various estimates of the gap between actual and potential GNP. Beginning year is 1949 for St. Louis "Fed" and "Trend" Gaps; 1955 for Perloff-Wachter Gap.

As shown in table 1.3, the rates of return on a posttax basis also have declined sharply in the 1970s, even after cyclical adjustment.

Another set of figures on trends in profitability are just as striking, if not more so, because the return on all assets is calculated, and, in addition, so-called inflation effects on the value of assets are incorporated. (This concept of total assets adjusts for inflation in the sense that tangible assets are priced at current cost and other assets would appear to be very close to current cost, e.g., receivables, etc.) A subsequent section in this chapter deals with the choice of the standard for judging rates of return, but figures on the return on total, rather than only depreciable, assets might also seem useful.

The rates of return in table 1.4, carry profits before taxes (NIPA) in the numerator and total assets (with depreciable assets in current values) in the denominator. These rates of return show 4.3 percent for the 1970-78 period, as compared with 7.0 percent as the long-term average in 1948-69. In the 1960s, this rate was 6.8 percent. (Here again, the issue of the inclusion of interest paid in the numerator of the rate of return arises.) The decline in posttax profitability is also evident — perhaps more distinctly on this basis.

SOME CAUSAL FACTORS

Several complex and interrelated factors have been active in generating the downdrift in rates of return which is evident in the profitability

Table 1.4. Nonfinancial Corporations
Rates of Return on Total Capital

Year Averages	(1) Profits Before Tax (NIPA)	(2) Net Interest	(3) Capital Income (1) + (2) (Bil. of Dol.)	(4) Total Assets*	(5) Rates of Return With Interest (Percent)	(6) Rates of Return Without Interest (Percent)
1948-78	54.3	10.5	64.8	998.3	7.3	6.2
1950-59	33.1	1.7	34.8	477.1	7.4	7.1
1960-69	56.9	6.7	63.6	835.4	7.6	6.8
1948-69	43.1	3.9	47.0	624.2	7.6	7.0
1970-78	81.7	26.6	108.3	1,912.9	5.7	4.3

Year Averages:	Profits After Tax (NIPA)	Net Interest	Capital Income (1) + (2) (Bil. of Dol.)	Total Assets*	Rates of Return With Interest (Percent)	Rates of Return Without Interest (Percent)
1948-78	26.6	10.5	37.6	998.3	3.8	3.1
1950-59	14.5	1.7	16.2	477.1	3.4	3.1
1960-69	31.2	6.7	38.0	835.4	4.5	3.7
1948-69	22.0	3.9	26.0	624.2	4.0	3.5
1970-78	37.9	26.6	64.5	1,912.9	3.4	2.0

*Tangible assets at current cost, financial assets at book value.
Source: Federal Reserve and Commerce Department.

measures. In the United States, as well as elsewhere among industrialized countries, important changes affecting productive inputs and, consequently, in the costs or incomes generated by employment of these factors have developed since the mid-1960s. This shift in relative costs was most dramatic in the 1970s, though it should be viewed as a continuum of important changes that began in the mid-1960s – prior to the dislocations generated by energy factors alone. Structural rather than cyclical forces apparently were at work, though some interaction must also have been involved.   Among the structural forces were changes in demographic composition of the labor force towards increased shares of less productive groups, technology shifts relating to energy and other factors, new environmental and safety requirements, etc. All contributed to lower productivity and higher costs, though incomplete price adjustments were made to these phenomena.

Possibly, these structural changes have not been given sufficient recognition as interim disequilibrium forces. That they appear to have had considerable staying power has been the major factor contributing to lowered rates of return. Some further explanation is warranted.

— The energy factor associated with the four-fold increase in crude oil prices since 1973 was a substantial element in raising real costs and in requiring expensive changes in technology in many industries. Ordinarily, profitability need not be affected by higher costs from this or any other source, as adjustments are made through the pricing process. This adjustment was delayed, or was simply not possible, for reasons discussed below. (In some studies, higher energy costs have been represented as a transient negative influence on profitability. But more than a transient influence apparently is involved, as has been the case with regard to other profit-reducing influences.

— An additional source of higher costs in recent years has been environmental and safety protection. Not only are decisions to allocate them as current or capital outlays difficult to make, but, in any event, they operate to diminish the productivity of capital outlays for the firm in the short-run, though social returns for the economy might be large over the longer term.
For nearly a decade, productivity growth in the private business sector appears to have declined — even prior to the effects occasioned by energy and other dislocations. Productivity growth averaged 2.7 percent per year in the 1960s and decreased to 1.3 percent in 1971-78, according to Department of Labor estimates. In the sophisticated econometrically-derived Perloff-Wachter estimates (1978), the decline in U.S. total long-term productivity, apart from cyclical influences, was measured as one-third — from 2.9 percent in the 1960s to 2.0 percent in the 1970s. Other studies support this conclusion (e.g., Kopcke, 1978). The secular decline in productivity clearly represents a force working towards reduced rates of return. It, too, poses the aforementioned problem of why ordinary market price adjustments have not been made.
No quick recovery from slower productivity growth may be expected over the next few years. It must be considered a negative structural element that will affect profitability for a while.

— Although other influences such as demographic and social factors also have contributed, the lessened pace of productivity must have developed in large part from a slow-up in growth of capital stock (4.3 percent annually in 1965-73, as compared with 2.4 percent in 1973-78). The slow-up in growth of capital appears as a secular or noncyclical phenomena. Note must be made, however, of recent studies which attribute only one-fourth to one-half of the shortfall in productivity growth to the slow-down in capital formation (Clark, 1977).

- Unit labor costs appeared to have entered a new phase of accelerated growth in the 1970s. Since this was not completely accommodated by price adjustment, rates of return were affected. As compared with average annual advances of 6 percent in hourly compensation during the 1960s, the rate increased to over 8 percent in the 1970s in the private sector – and, indeed, was just under 10 percent during 1974-77. Unit labor costs had advanced at an annual rate of only 2.5 percent in the 1960s and increased to a rate of 6 percent in the 1970s.

- As a consequence of these developments, the real cost of compensation for labor, relative to most property income returns, appears to have increased since the mid-1960s. While the share of wage and salary payments has remained relatively stable, that of fringe benefits has registered sharp growth. (In the 1960s, by contrast, the rapid expansion of economic activity was accompanied by a larger share of corporate product accruing to property incomes.)
Despite lower productivity in the 1970s, the labor compensation share of corporate product has advanced markedly – averaging 66.7 percent in 1970-78, as compared with 64.3 percent in 1960-69. By contrast, the profit margin in 1970-78 – profits before tax (NIPA) as a percentage of corporate product – averaged 9.6 percent, as compared with 14.7 percent in 1960-69. In 1976-78, the margin rose to 10.2 percent, little different from the earlier 1970s, despite the economic recovery.
The decline in the profit share of output might be said to reflect, in part, some variation in capital-output ratios. However, if it is assumed that no significant trend in these ratios has developed, then the profit share movement becomes significant. (If capital intensity were to increase, rates of return might decline even without the push from higher labor compensation.)

The inflation of the 1970s has shifted cost and income shares, though in a fashion which conventional economic theory would not have predicted. Conventional thought casts profit takers in the role of "inflation-gainers" and wage earners as "inflation-losers." The opposite seems to have occurred in the 1970s (see fig. 1.2).

Against these perspectives, it remains a matter of hypothesis with respect to why the usual market processes have not worked to restore equilibrium in income shares and to regain more adequate rates of return. Indeed, because of new uncertainties generated by inflation, environment requirements, etc., a premium in rates of return may now be needed to promote investment – the "target rate" of return may have been raised.

Another view of the incomplete adjustment of rates of return is that the inflation, accelerated though it has been in recent years, might have been insufficient to regain a balance of relative real inputs that is as favorable to corporate ownership as was formerly evident. Whatever the causes of incomplete adjustment for the United States – more

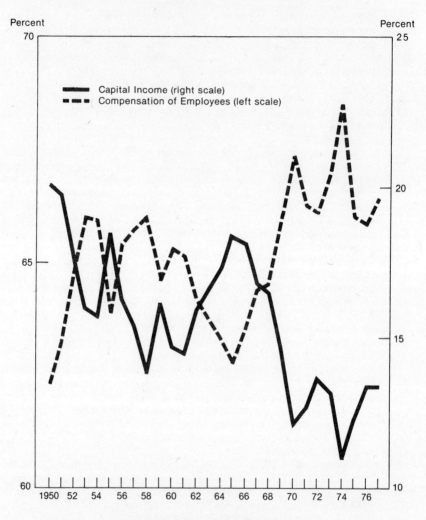

Note: Capital income is profits before taxes (NIPA) plus net interest paid.

Fig. 1.2. Shares of compensation of employees and profits plus
interest in nonfinancial corporate product.

intense international competition, the drag on prices from excess
capacity for some materials, anxiety concerning a possible backlash
from government through price controls or other means — a lag has
developed in adjustment of total receipts from dislocations in factor
costs. That is to say, market prices have not yet adjusted to the new
equilibrium. Figures 1.3 and 1.4 suggest, by visual inspection, that the
profit share of GNP is in disequilibrium.

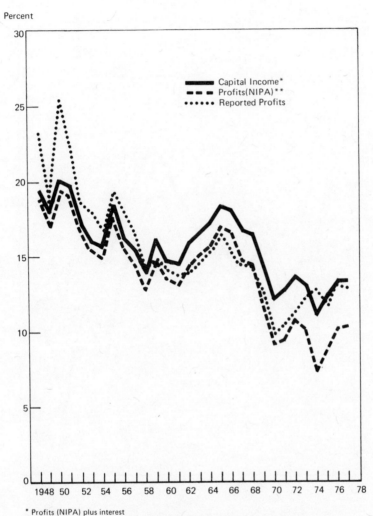

Percent

* Profits (NIPA) plus interest
** Reported profits with IVA plus Capital Consumption Adjustment

Fig. 1.3. Capital income, profits (NIPA), and reported profits before tax as a percentage of nonfinancial gross corporate product.

However, the econometric analysis (which is contained in the Statistical Appendix) also support the conclusion of lowered profitability. While the equations do not hypothesize causes of profitability, they do quantify the influence of several types of "pressure variables" and of time trends.

The following generalizations concerning profitability may be drawn from the accompanying figures and the equations in the Statistical Appendix:

Percent

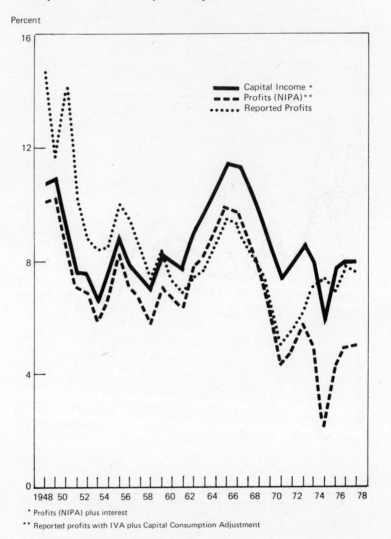

* Profits (NIPA) plus interest

** Reported profits with IVA plus Capital Consumption Adjustment

Fig. 1.4. Capital income, profits (NIPA), and reported profits
after tax as a percentage of nonfinancial gross corporate product.

– Rates of return on investment, defined in terms of either pretax
or posttax profits (NIPA) in the numerator and total physical
reproducible capital in the denominator, in the 1970s were below
long-term postwar averages and well below those in the mid-
1960s. (See figs. 1.5 and 1.6).

– Adding net interest paid on top of profits ("capital income") to the numerator modifies this pattern, but does not change its direction. (See fig. 1.7.)

- Rates of return on net worth, as an alternative measure, also follow this pattern. (Indeed, as fig. 1.8 shows, profitability measures based on net worth of depreciable assets are so close that separate regression analysis for net worth was not deemed necessary.)

- Though less reliable, a standard, cyclically adjusted profitability exhibits a similar downtrend for the 1970s. The several new and uniformly lower measures of potential GNP that have become available lessen the value of the cyclical adjustments that are required and reduce the margin between actual and adjusted rates of return. Lowered profitability in the U.S. over the long term will persist even under conditions of so-called "full employment".

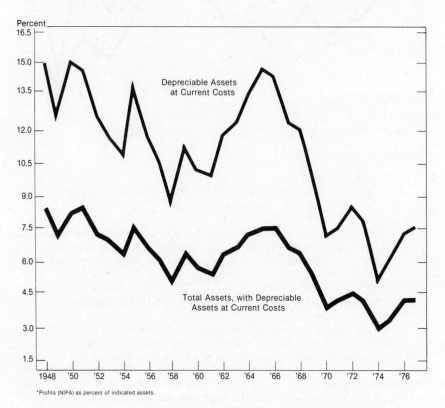

*Profits (NIPA) as percent of indicated assets.

Fig. 1.5. Nonfinancial corporations: rates of return on profits before tax (NIPA).*

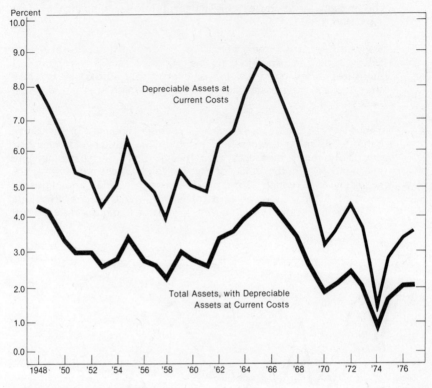

*Profits (NIPA) as percent of indicated assets

Fig. 1.6. Nonfinancial corporations: rates of return on profits
after tax (NIPA).*

- Profits calculated as a percent of gross product also appear to
have lessened in recent years. (See fig. 1.3). Despite inflation,
profit margins appear squeezed, unlike traditional expectations.

"INFLATION-ADJUSTED" RESULTS: MYTH OR REALITY?

As noted earlier, a large but controversial literature has emerged which
features a procedure whereby windfall gains attained by a reduction in
the real value of corporate debt as a result of inflation are added to
profits. Of course, this is a "holding gain" rather than "operating
income" and, hence, says little concerning the incentive to invest. Still,
adding these windfalls to profits does change the general contours of
the decline in rates of return ascribed to the 1970s.

Some principal technical difficulties in these estimates are the
varying maturity of the debt held by corporations (gains would apply
only to long-term debt); and which price level deflator to use in

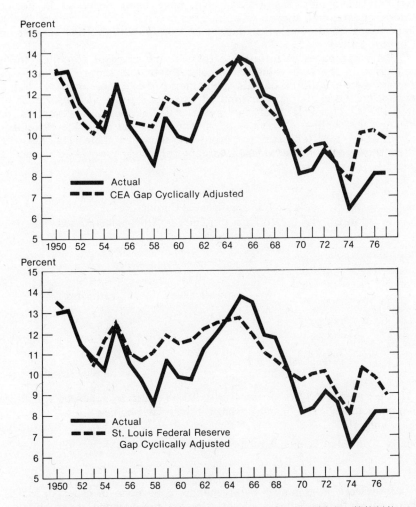

Fig. 1.7. Rates of return on profits before tax (NIPA) plus interest, nonfinancial corporations: actual and cyclically adjusted.

calculating the purchasing power of the profit dollar. And, to the extent that inflation has been anticipated by investors, a "double count" is difficult to avoid; this already may have been reflected in higher interest costs, and, therefore in lowered profits. (Further review of the importance of the inflation impact on corporate liabilities appears in Chapter 5.)

Some estimates of inflation effects which attempt to adjust for a reduction in the real value of corporate debt are shown in table 1.5. Assuming the validity of this adjustment, they, too, indicate that a decline in these officially estimated rates of return was registered in the 1970s. The effect of the inflation adjustment, however, is to dampen the decline. (A compendium of the several available estimates of inflation adjusted rates of return are shown in table D12. Most of them show peaks in the middle 1960s and relatively low values in recent years.)

Table 1.5. Nonfinancial Corporations:
"Inflation Adjusted Rates of Return on Stockholders' Equity
(percent)

| | Published[a] | |
	1978 Estimates	1979 Estimates
1955-59	5.18	4.94
1960-69	6.54	6.90
1970-77[b]	5.61	5.84

[a]After-tax profits (NIPA) corrected for inflation effects by application of change in manufacturers' prices on outstanding net financial liabilities.
[b]Excluding 1974.

Source: Council of Economic Advisors.

More work in this area surely needs to be done in order to assess more carefully the impact of inflation on the balance sheet and the income statement. The inflation adjustments are very fragile, both conceptually and statistically. (They are discussed subsequently in Chapter 3.) Conventional accounting systems, from which profitability measures ultimately are derived in the national accounts, have become increasingly deceptive – depending as they do largely on historical rather than replacement costs and values. In a world of accelerating inflation, valuations of assets, liabilities, and current costs are difficult to determine, making the investment decision particularly fragile. The results of this and other investigations in this area must be considered tentative.

Percent

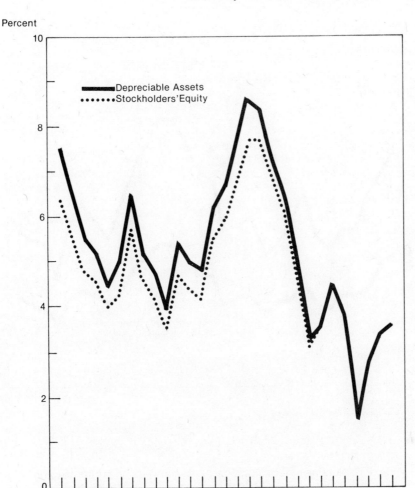

Fig. 1.8. Profits after tax (NIPA) as a percent of depreciable assets
and of stockholders equity.

THE CHOICE OF A PROFITABILITY STANDARD: A PREVIEW

Theoretically, the choice of a standard of profitability would appear to
be crucial in determining the trend in rates of return during recent
years. Indeed, the literature features many controversies and suggestions concerning the need for this or that type of adjustment towards
the attainment of some optimal standard of profitability. However,
those controversies do not appear to have made much difference to the
general conclusion of this study; notably, that behind the veil of real or

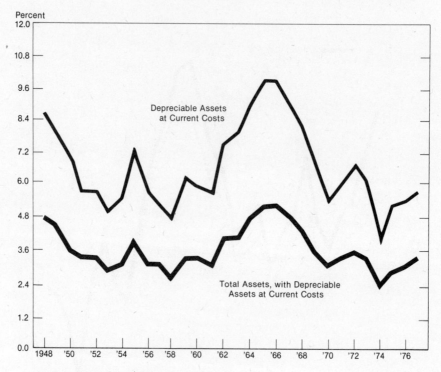

Fig. 1.9. Nonfinancial corporations: rates of return on profits after tax
(NIPA) plus interest.*

contrived controversy over the choice of a standard, rates of return appear to have declined in the 1970s.

The conclusions of this study differed from those that indicated no downtrend in probitability because of a) the nature of the cyclical adjustments, b) the time trend analysis which places the 1970s in a more "normal" perspective, and c) the greater significance placed on the apparent squeeze in profit margins, as reflected in inadequate adjustment to the rising labor compensation share in corporate gross national product.

Moreover, it appeared to make little difference in the results of the regression analysis, with respect to general trends, regarding which of the alternative concepts was used in the numerator and denominator in calculating rates of return. In the numerator, rates of return were

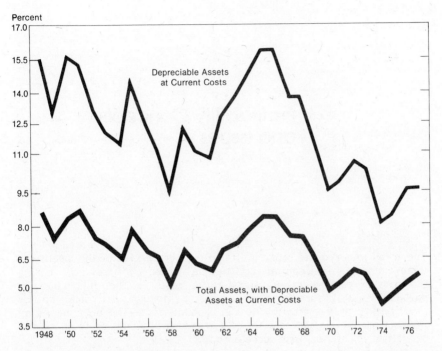

Percent

*Capital income (NIPA) as percent of indicated assets.

Fig. 1.10. Nonfinancial corporations: rates of return on profits before tax (NIPA) plus interest.*

calculated using profits before and after taxes or with and without interest paid. The principal concern about the appropriate concept was the use of economic profits as defined in the national accounts, which makes adjustments for the replacement of cost of inventory and depreciation. The inclusion or exclusion of interest is more controversial, with many arguing for inclusion on the basis that the form of financing of assets should not influence a calculation of rates of return on capital. Still, a downward trend in profitability on "capital income" was also observable, as summarized in preceding pages.

What seemed decisive for this study's selection of a standard was the little difference it made in the results, except for levels, with respect to the variation in the parameter used in the denominator of the rate of return calculation – depreciable assets at current cost, total assets at current costs (tangible assets at current cost plus financial assets), or net worth. This is depicted in figure 1.8, which shows the nearly identical movement in rates of return based on depreciable assets, and on stockholders' equity. This is also evident in trends shown in figures 1.9 and 1.10.

2 Profitability Concepts and Issues

The trend in corporate profitability in the perspective of the incentives to invest in physical capital facilities has become a lively issue during the past several years. Its significance rests on the importance of physical capital formation as a major (though not sole) factor contributing to the growth rate of productivity – the only means by which a nation can increase its own standard of living or to share the benefit, if it chooses, with those abroad.

Moreover, national goals of high employment and low rates of inflation in the United States – and avoidance of the stagflation problem – are directly associated with adequacy of investment: new plants and other physical facilities create new demands for labor; while the increased ability to produce works to moderate the inflationary pressures from the supply side. In addition, increased production made possible from capital formation and lowered unit costs should increase the international competitiveness of the U.S.

Missing full advantage of these benefits, the "full employment-unemployment rate" has been raised, in part reflecting the decline in growth of the ratio of fixed capital stock to the labor force from over two percent a year in the 1950s and 1960s to little growth since 1973. Associated with this circumstance has been the advent of lowered labor productivity in the United States – from annual growth of 2.5 percent or so in the earlier postwar period to one-third that since 1973.

Finally, aside from these macroeconomic effects, productivity and economic growth create the environment and resources for dealing with microeconomic structural and welfare problems of the economy – those relating to an improved functioning of our labor markets that will better the mix of available jobs and job skills, provide social and economic benefits to those unable to sustain themselves economically, and serve the general public's need for social amenities, safety, and environmental benefits.

Clearly, public policies need to be directed, if they are not already so, towards the nurture of capital formation and its potential benefits, important as they appear to be. Of course, that need not consist of direct intervention by the government – perhaps that influence already may have misdirected the flow of resources. But its role needs to be ascertained, within the scope of this study.

A prior condition to attain these benefits is the volume of resources that might be placed in capital formation. Indeed, the issue has been raised that the United States saves too little; that undersaving or overconsumption has been the American predisposition; that gross business fixed investment as a share of domestic product in the United States ranks lowest among major industrial nations – 14 percent versus an average of about 19 percent for the 11 OECD countries.

This lower share, of course, is characteristic of the United States in the postwar period, though it carries greater significance as a contributor to inflation than formerly. Moreover, the share has diminished on balance in recent years, especially when allowance is made for environmental and safety outlays. Whether this is a permanent or temporary decline hinges on many considerations. But, trends in rates of return appear to have played an important role in these developments, both in the short and long run.

Of course, it has been argued that the free play of economic forces would result eventually in raising capital formation if the endogenously-stimulated signals so directed the flow of resources. As they developed, higher rates of return to investment would encourage more saving or channel it to sectors of relatively high investment demand. But, this appears so only if rates of return or rewards to savers have fully adjusted to market conditions, which are assumed, in this argument, to be free of rigidities or institutional or governmental regulatory impediments; and, in recent years, of major uncertainties caused by inflation which are not reflected fully in interest rate adjustments between lenders and borrowers. This study will suggest that rates of return to corporate enterprise have been lower than they otherwise would have been, due to these factors.

It has also been said that neither greater productive capacity nor increased productivity is relevant to attain high employment without undue inflation. High employment, of course, may be secured by other means – though it surely would be less productive on these terms and, hence, more conducive to inflation and lower growth in living standards. And, while it is true that increased investment temporarily may increase demand more than supply, that would not be a long-run development, provided capacity eventually increased.

CHANNELING RESOURCES INTO SAVING

Even though expansion in investment would contribute substantially to increased living standards and lower inflation, there still remain many issues to be resolved. Probably most important are the factors which govern the incentive to invest and the means which are available to finance increased investment. Only major considerations will be noted in this study, which focuses on corporate rates of return and their relation to capital formation. As summarized in chapter 1, the contention of this study is that corporate rates of return appear to have diminished in recent years, contributing to insufficient rates of investment and making difficult the attainment of the aforementioned goals.

Granted that investment incentives are strongly connected with sufficiency of markets, as Eisner (1969) and others have argued with great cogency; and, as facilities are expanded to meet market demand, the additional investment spending ramifies into increased national product and incomes. And granted, also, that there is generated, thereby, greater personal and corporate saving which provides the financing that facilitates the apparent endogenously inspired process of saving and investment. In this context, both uses and sources of funds appear to proceed hand-in-hand down an untroubled primrose path.

But, this process would appear to be more relevant to the short run or under circumstances of less than full employment, indeed, emerging only under conditions when real resources are less than fully utilized. Actually, the economy's performance in the postwar period might be characterized as a time of generally high levels of economic activity which has been interrupted by brief, albeit sometimes sharp, recessions. At the higher levels of economic activity, the automatic generation of corporate saving to finance investment may not be endogenously inspired, as described earlier.

In fact, the economy, as it approaches full utilization of real resources, then stands at a crossroads. On an assumption of relatively full utilization of resources, there is no escape from the issue of some optimum or socially desirable balance between consumption and saving. Presently, the United States appears tilted toward the former.

While this decision of allocation of resources between consumption and saving is made primarily by consumer and investor preferences in the United States, the market would work the problem in the context of already existing institutional controls, including tax and other economic policies. In this perspective, the choice between a high consumption-low saving versus a low consumption-high saving economy might be influenced by economic policy, and would bring in its wake important consequences with respect to standards of living and inflation. Under circumstances of high activity, the decision to invest, that is to say, to substitute future for current consumption, becomes crucial to the economy. That decision could be strongly influenced by rates of return that induce deferral of consumption. Private saving would be encouraged only if it were deemed worth the candle. Anticipating a conclusion of this study, economic and social policy in the United States would appear to need reformulation towards greater rewards to savers and investors.

WHICH RATE OF RETURN?

Complicated and uncertain as they always were, the standard measures of corporate profitability remain so, despite much attention. Even prior to the era of sharply rising prices, which has made more difficult the interpretation of historically based figures reported in income statements and balance sheets, there existed many profound problems in defining profit. No standard meaning has emerged, though many companies both in the United States and abroad appear to have followed the principle that "it may usefully be defined as the amount of the total gains arising in a year that may prudently be regarded as distributable. . . . (leaving the company) as well off in the end of the year as it was at the beginning" (Sandilands, 1975, pp. 28-29). Aside from the problem of distinguishing "holding" versus "operating" gains, at least five possible concepts of profit have been discerned by some authorities (Sandilands, 1975); and that represents only the views of one eminent committee.

The determination of "economic income and profits is difficult, if only from the basic condition that the statistical raw materials that contribute to the national figures on revenues and costs are derived from conventional accounting records. Accounting conventions may not accord with economic concepts; such issues intervene as accrual versus cash income; nominal versus "effective" tax rates; etc. Again, the proper consideration of costs is not simple: decisions must be made to accept or reject historical or replacement costs of assets and alternative methods of depreciation. Finally, such issues as the capitalization of research and development expenditures or advertising outlays become too complicated even to warrant entry into serious public debate.

Those issues were joined by a new set of problems affecting measurements in both the income statement and the balance sheet. The problems were generated by accelerated inflation since the mid-1960s. Additional consideration of inflation and its impact on conventionally measured profits, assets, and liabilities is given in Chapter 3. See especially the treatment by Cagan and Lipsey (1978) and by Kopcke (1979). This study owes much to Kopcke's quantifications in refutation of the notion that inflation has benefited corporate rates of return.

Among the imagined or real impacts of inflation are gains and losses accruing to a firm as a result of changes in the market value of debt, to the extent that prices and interest rate changes are unanticipated. Since nonfinancial corporations are net debtors, it is argued that under inflationary conditions a capital gain on debt has accrued that should be added to profits.

This is in contrast with conventional theory whereby contracts made under "anticipated" inflation conditions allow for depreciation of dollar-determined assets in such manner that all real values remain unchanged. Neither debtors nor creditors would gain, except temporarily. In the limit, economic behavior and decisions affecting the allocation of resources are thought to remain unchanged. On the balance sheet, a shift occurs from those assets on which inflation wreaks damage (fixed claim assets) to those of variable claims which raise the valuation of real estate, stocks, etc. Rates of return among these assets get realigned; the rising cost of holding money, which is being depreciated, is offset by monetary gains from higher interest rates.

The period since the mid-1960s however, has been characterized by uninterrupted as well and more than anticipated rates of inflation. As a result, disequilibrium in terms of shifts among assets has not equalized rates of return. A major example in recent years has been the decline in the stock market, formerly considered a major hedge against inflation. Conventional theory presumes that profits, at least initially, should become the prime beneficiary of inflation. This should have been reflected in higher equity prices.

Circumstances, however, have not followed this pattern. Stock market values have not exhibited the typical upswing of a business expansion — which has led some to believe (Malkiel, 1977) that a stock market boom in the period ahead may be expected to develop. That prospect does not meet the expectations implied in this study, due to the structural factors discussed in Chapter 1.

An essential element in this puzzle points to the investor's preference for one of the several estimates of earnings streams that might point to later performance. The major issues that have influenced these figures are:

— The adjustment to profits required to convert historically-costed inventories and depreciation to replacement cost. The effect of these adjustments, which are described below, is to raise the effective tax rate and thereby lower after tax returns on investment.

— The revaluation of financial and nonfinancial assets and liabilities in reaction to the inflation. These effects, taken in totality of reduced obligations to creditors and increased obligations to pension funds, has not benefited from inflation.

— Profit margins have been squeezed, as inadequate adjustment developed in relation to rising shares of labor compensation.

Theoretically, the profitability of all capital is determined by the return on marginal investments. In perfect markets, a single rate of return under equilibrium conditions will equate the demand for and supply of capital goods. Departures from equilibrium to a low rate of return provide an indication that additional investment will also carry a low return. Conversely, a high rate of return suggests that new investment will also share this characteristic. Accordingly, the existing data on profitability are useful as indicators of the returns that are likely for new investment.

INCOME STATEMENTS AND INFLATION ACCOUNTING

At least two concepts of corporate profits are in common use: 1) conventional or "book profits" which typically reflect historical costs, and 2) economic profits — earnings which have been adjusted for the effects of changing prices on inventories and capital consumption allowances. This is sometimes called "operating profits." Other concepts, such as those developed by Cagan and Lipsey (1978), which make inflation adjustments to profits due to revaluation of assets and liabilities, are recent and controversial approaches.

The basic principles involved in the proper adjustment of corporate profits during inflationary times have been the subject of many contributions including Terborgh (1974), Shoven and Bulow (1975), Tideman and Tucker (1976 and Aaron (1976). These studies seek to measure effects on reported corporate profits arising from the use of historical rather than replacement costs in computing depreciation allowances and inventory profits. Though the inventory valuation adjustment had been adopted several decades ago, the 1976 revision of the National Income and Product Accounts (NIPA) gave additional prominence to profits adjusted for the biases due to historical cost depreciation. Since the methods used in calculating NIPA profits have generated some controversy, a brief discussion of the conceptual underpinnings of Inventory Valuation Adjustment (IVA) and Capital Consumption Adjustment (CCA) is appropriate.

Inventory Profits

A consensus appears to have emerged regarding the appropriate treatment of inventory profits – those that accrue simply because prices have increased since the period when stocks were purchased or used in production. The conceptually ideal – but not practically feasible – way of measuring inventory profits would be to compute the gain on each item sold as its price, less its current cost of production (or purchase, in the instance of finished goods in trade companies). Two inventory accounting procedures based on different assumptions of timing of costs are in common use. The FIFO – or first in, first out accounting procedure – stipulates that the cost of goods sold is computed as if they were the oldest goods in inventory. The replacement cost of materials entering into current sales is neglected and profits are thereby overstated during periods of inflation. In LIFO accounting – last in, first out – the cost of goods most recently inventoried, is charged against revenues. In inflationary times, the former method leads to higher reported "book profits." This procedure would disregard the fact that such inventory profits will be required to replace inventories; they would not be available for distribution to stockholders. Since the firm cannot replenish its inventories at less than current costs, LIFO accounting is a common method of pricing inventories that would be necessary to avoid counting as profits that are based on unrealistic historical cost.

(Use of LIFO does not eliminate inventory profits completely, as when a product line is being dropped or a business lowers or discontinues operations and thereby utilizes older and less costly inventory that does not need to be replaced.)

Under Internal Revenue Service regulations, companies may elect to calculate profits under any of several methods, including FIFO and

LIFO, though they may not shift arbitrarily. While FIFO continues in widespread use, many firms have recently switched to LIFO in order to reduce tax liabilities. Official NIPA profits figures are calculated by adding the inventory valuation adjustment (IVA) to reported book profits. Essentially, the NIPA procedure reconstructs profits on a LIFO basis to account for the replacement cost of inventory. A large effect may ensue: in 1974, when inflation accelerated sharply, the IVA was $40.4 billion. The size of the IVA can be expected to decline as more firms shift to LIFO accounting.

Capital Consumption

A second important impact of inflation on accounting figures concerns the capital consumption allowance for depreciable assets. Since depreciation is conventionally calculated on an historic cost basis, a period of rising prices would raise the replacement cost of capital goods, but not the value of depreciation allowances if historical cost was retained as an accounting procedure. Profits would then be exaggerated, because the costs of replacing capital goods used up in production are understated.

A second issue affecting depreciation cost relates to the economic service or useful life of an asset, as distinguished from its taxable life, which depends on the corporate choice of straight-line or other favored form of depreciation. In the 1976 NIPA revision, the capital consumption adjustment (CCA) was introduced. In this procedure, depreciation reported for tax purposes is converted to the appropriate replacement cost basis — taking into account changes in the prices of capital goods, as well as depreciation cost based on economic rather than tax service lives. The adjustment can be quite large, reaching $17.7 billion in 1978. It is important to note that the size of the CCA depends critically on past as well as the current rate of inflation. Even if the current rate of inflation should subside, depreciation allowances for tax purposes will remain too low, in an economic sense, for some time to come.

The CCA assumes that the economic service lives of depreciable assets are realistically described by straight-line depreciation of 85 percent of the service lives of specific assets indicated by Bulletin F of the Internal Revenue Service. This has led Terborgh (1978) to reaffirm that the CCA as officially reported is inadequate. He prefers to rely on an alternate calculation, also made by the Department of Commerce, which is based on estimates of double declining balance depreciation. Unfortunately, insufficient information exists to allow a definitive choice between the two depreciation methods. (For this reason, the econometric analysis on rates of returning which are shown in the Statistical Appendix, utilize both depreciation methods in the profit variables.

The important effect of the CCA and IVA on reported profits for selected years is shown in table 2.1. On the double-digit inflation period of 1974, the inflation adjustments reduce before-tax profits by 42 percent, while after-tax profits are cut by 72 percent. Currently, "phantom" aspects account for about 43 percent of total posttax profits.

Table 2.1. Nonfinancial Corporations:
The Simple Effect of Inflation on Reported Profits

Year	Unadjusted Pretax Profits	Unadjusted Posttax Profits	Inflation Adjustment (IVA+CCA)	Share of Inflationary Profit, Pretax (3) ÷ (1)	Share of Inflationary Profit, Posttax (3) ÷ (2)
		(Billions of Dol.)		(Percent)	
	(1)	(2)	(3)	(4)	(5)
1950	38.5	21.6	-8.9	.231	.412
1955	42.0	21.8	-3.8	.090	.174
1960	39.5	20.3	-2.0	.051	.099
1965	64.4	37.2	1.7	.026	.046
1970	55.1	27.9	-3.6	.065	.129
1973	92.7	53.1	-16.8	.181	.316
1974	102.9	60.2	-43.4	.422	.721
1975	101.3	60.7	-24.3	.240	.400
1976	130.2	77.2	-28.8	.220	.393
1977	143.5	84.5	-29.5	.206	.349
1978	167.0	98.4	-42.0	.251	.427

THE BALANCE SHEET, THE INCOME STATEMENT, AND INFLATION

Profits might also be viewed in the context of those changes in the balance sheet which represent holding gains or losses on assets and liabilities, as recorded or estimated by accountants or economists for inflation impacts. Returns to equity holders may be adjusted to reflect gains from the reduced burden of liabilities resulting from higher prices, as well as higher capital consumption allowances that reflect upward-valued physical assets. Since most corporations are net debtors, they and their shareholders experience gains on two accounts. First, outstanding debt is easier to repay as prices rise; and second, a capital gain, whether realized or not, might be recorded since rising interest rates lower the value of debt securities. (The latter is considered a controversial adjustment, as Chapter 3 indicates.) This decline in the burden occurs because the higher interest rates which accompany increased inflation necessarily leads to reductions in bond prices. In other words, the real value of the debt has diminished, even if it should not have been realized by actual repurchase.

The following example, which takes taxes into account, is further illustrative. Suppose a corporation is able to borrow at four percent in a situation of no inflation. Since interest costs are deductible from profits, the 48 percent marginal corporate tax rate applicable in 1978 would reduce borrowing costs to about two percent. If the expected rate of inflation rises to four percent, then the corporation would borrow at an eight percent interest rate. But, the deduction of about four percent would make the after-tax cost of borrowing four percent – exactly equal to the rate of inflation. The real cost of borrowing would be zero. Inflation would have reduced the tax burden at the corporate level on debt-financed investment.

Unlike the inventory and capital consumption adjustments, the debt adjustments in reaction to inflation may not affect the return to the total suppliers of capital. The gain to equity owners eventually may be offset by an equal and opposite loss to bond owners. This makes it unlikely that the gains will persist, unless unexpected inflation persists. Bond holders will require higher yields to compensate for high inflation. Indeed, an increase in inflation raises profits by bringing about a capital gain on old debt, which may be temporary. No capital gain on debt arises from the finance of new investment projects, since it must be issued at the new higher interest rates.

THE HOLDING GAIN ON DEBT AND PENSION RESERVES

The lightened debt burden of corporations due to unexpected inflation may have been exaggerated by Cagan and Lipsey (1978), Shoven and Bulow (1975) and the Council of Economic Advisors (1979). Two benefits have been differentiated: 1) a reduction in the real burden of debt repayment because dollars have depreciated and 2) the lowered market price of debt which occurs when interest rates rise (which reduces the value of liabilities and hence raises net worth). Rates of return for corporations are thereby increased because the tax saving from exclusion of real gains on the debt is sufficient to offset the excess tax caused by the mismeasurement of depreciation and inventory profits.

These gains may be illusory, in part or whole, due to holding losses on debt in corporate pension plans. Pension liabilities rise when compensation of labor increases. As the latter responds to inflation catch-up requirements, the earlier commitments to fund pension liabilities prove to be too small, generating a drain on income or an increase in unfunded liabilities. Because pension reserves are frequently placed in long-term bonds, the yield on the outstanding amount will not have kept pace with the inflation; and so the corporation will be confronted with increased liabilities. This holding loss has not been accounted for in the studies presently available.

Long-term debt held by pension funds amounts to about one-half of the value of nonfinancial corporate business' long-term debt. In effect, stockholders become "creditors," who share the losses on outstanding debt due to inflation. Stockholder obligations swell whenever the inflation rate increases more than was expected. An unfunded pension liability arises because the present value of pension liabilities exceeds accumulated reserves. For example, with a 2 percent inflation rate, a typical fully funded pension plan holds assets of sufficiently high yield to provide adequate financing for the vested retirement obligations of the firm. Should the inflation rate unexpectedly increase to 6 percent, the future benefits promised by the firm increase substantially . . . but the assets of the plan are now locked into securities with relatively low and inadequate yields (Kopcke, 1979).

Another aspect of this issue relates to those pension reserves that are invested in equity, which comprise about one-half of pension reserves. As long as equity values fail to keep pace with wages, pension fund assets decline in relative value, posing new obligations upon the corporation.

The net impact of these factors – gains on outstanding debt and losses on pension fund assets and other equities – is difficult to assess. There may have been little net gain at all from unexpected inflation on debt. Indeed, some estimates of unfunded liabilities show that pension fund losses exceed the gain on debt.

Loss from long term debt in creditor status is only part of unfunded liability that may arise and which will lower rates of return for corporations. As inflation and other factors eroded after-tax earnings of corporations, and the value of equities declined, new sources of unfunded liabilities have emerged. As unanticipated inflation developed, stockholders' responsibilities to maintain the purchasing power guarantee to pension funds are increased; and equity values tend to decline to reflect their share of unfunded pension liabilities.

THE "SOCIAL RETURN" TO CAPITAL

While most recent studies of profitability have emphasized the rate of return to private investors, attention has also focused on the "social return" to capital. It is the "social return," the sum of the return to private investors and to the government in the form of taxes, which influences the decision to invest and to secure increased capital formation. A useful framework for distinguishing pretax social return and the posttax private rates of return may be found in Feldstein (1977).

He argues that the pretax rate of return reflects the full social product of capital, and that this figure should guide decisions regarding capital formation. Feldstein and Summers write,

> Our . . . purpose is to provide an estimate of the return that the nation can earn on additional private corporate investments. The national rate of return on private investment should be a key to the question of whether the rate of capital accumulation is 'too low.' It should also be the critical parameter in the cost-benefit analysis of projects that diverts funds from private investment through either borrowing or taxation. As such, the estimated pretax return on private investment should influence energy and environmental policy (1977, p. 212).

Feldstein indicates that it is the pre- rather than the posttax rate of return which properly measures the return to capital formation. However, it is clear from his discussion that he views the posttax return as the relevant variable if the private incentive to invest is at issue.

Indeed, much of his argument is directed at showing that because taxes drive a wedge between the private and social returns to investment, they create a prima facie case that the national rate of investment is too low.

MEASURING THE CAPITAL STOCK

In many studies, the rate of return calculated for nonfinancial corporations depends on some measure of profits in the numerator and the value of the physical capital stock in the denominator -- either with or without the value of land. Capital stock estimation involves many of the same issues and difficulties as profit determination, such as adjustment of the depreciation allowance into replacement cost terms. Estimates of the size of the capital stock must take into consideration its three major nonfinancial components: fixed reproducible capital, inventories, and land.

Estimates of the physical reproducible capital stock, including inventories on a replacement cost basis, are now available for the nonfinancial corporate sector from the Department of Commerce (Survey of Current Business, March 1976,) and subsequent issues. They have provided a strong statistical base for calculating rates of return. However, they are not flawless because they embody the concept of straight-line depreciation, which has not been generally accepted as realistic. Moreover, use of 85% of service-life in IRS's Bulletin F has been challenged.

Estimates of the value of land held in the nonfinancial corporate sector have diverged widely in various studies. As a result, several analysts (e.g., Nordhaus, 1974) have set aside this component of physical assets. When eliminated, estimated rates of return are obviously higher, though trends over time may not be affected. Omission of land raises the level of estimated rates of profit by about 20 percent or more.

TAXES AND PROFITABILITY

Disagreement concerning trends in profitability results from the use of pretax earnings in some studies and posttax returns in others. The discussion in the section on the "social return to investment" describes the quite different reasons for studying the various concepts. Trends in profitability may vary because of changes in the share of equity and debt financing of corporate investment; and increases in the effective tax rate on the corporate income resulting from inflation. Therefore, pre- and posttax rates of profit have behaved somewhat differently over the postwar period. Much has been made of this in some studies (though this study has concluded otherwise).

Of major significance to profit trends has been this rise in effective tax rates. These have increased in recent years, even while legislation permitted investment tax credits and lowered official corporate rates. Primarily due to the inflation, the decline in the effective tax rate

Table 2.2. Effective Tax Rates, Nonfinancial Corporations

	Profits Before Tax (NIPA)	Taxes Paid	Profits After Tax (NIPA)	Effective Tax Rate	Maximum Tax Rate*
	billion dollars			percent	
1948	25.8	11.8	14.0	45.7	38.0
1949	23.0	9.3	13.7	40.7	38.0
1950	29.6	16.9	12.7	57.1	42.0
1951	33.4	21.2	12.2	63.5	50.75
1952	30.3	17.8	12.5	58.7	52.0
1953	29.9	18.5	11.4	61.9	52.0
1954	28.6	15.6	13.0	54.5	52.0
1955	38.2	20.2	18.0	52.9	52.0
1956	36.1	20.1	16.0	55.7	52.0
1957	35.0	19.1	15.9	54.6	52.0
1958	30.1	16.2	13.9	53.8	52.0
1959	39.7	20.7	19.0	52.1	52.0
1960	37.4	19.2	18.3	51.3	52.0
1961	37.4	19.5	17.9	52.1	52.0
1962	44.9	20.6	24.3	45.9	52.0
1963	50.0	22.8	27.2	45.6	52.0
1964	56.7	24.0	32.7	42.3	50.0
1965	66.1	27.2	38.9	41.1	48.0
1966	71.2	29.5	41.7	41.4	48.0
1967	67.2	27.7	39.5	41.2	48.0
1968	72.1	33.6	38.5	46.6	52.8
1969	66.4	33.3	33.1	50.2	52.8
1970	51.6	27.3	24.3	52.9	49.2
1971	58.7	29.9	28.8	50.9	48.6
1972	72.0	33.5	38.5	46.5	48.0
1973	76.0	39.6	36.4	52.1	48.0
1974	59.5	42.7	16.8	71.8	48.0
1975	76.9	40.6	36.3	52.8	48.0
1976	101.3	53.0	48.3	52.3	48.0
1977	113.9	59.0	54.9	51.8	48.0
1978	125.1	68.6	56.5	54.8	48.0

*Tax rate applicable to large corporations, where income generally exceeds $25,000.

halted in the mid-1960s and has trended up since that time, as shown in table 2.2. (Surely, it has been a factor in the negative time trend on profit rates that this study has found.)

CYCLICAL ADJUSTMENTS

The data on profits, improved though they may be in the national accounts for economic analysis, need to be cyclically adjusted to uncover secular trends. However, the magnitude of cyclical adjustment depends critically on a "full" or "high" employment potential GNP construct, from which actual GNP is subtracted to obtain a "gap." The latter then is used as the cyclical (or pressure) variable: the larger the "gap", the greater the raising factor on profit rates required to discern secular trend.

However, that measure is subject to more than the usual statistical difficulties, as discussed subsequently. Indeed, the several such estimates of potential GNP and the gap differ significantly. Accordingly, estimates of cyclically adjusted profitability also differ, as the analysis will show.

3 Which Way Profitability: Survey of the Recent Literature

Detailed consideration was given in Chapter 2 to the many problems associated with definitions of profits and profitability viewed as a rate of return. These problems have led to alternate approaches in the many studies that have dealt with corporate rates of return. The choice, of course, in these prior studies depended upon the specific problem that was being addressed — trends in growth of property income, incentives to invest by individuals and corporations (together or separately), the ability to expand corporate activity (which might argue for retained earnings or cash flow in the numerator), etc.

Among earlier studies in the 1950s and 1960s, the ratio of profits to net worth was frequently utilized, despite differences among the firm's accounts that would arise from variation in financing methods as between equity and debt. Moreover, inflation impacts on profits (a current flow) would be different than those on net worth (a stock), thereby overlooking the higher current prices of physical assets that would preserve symmetry in valuations of the numerator and denominator. Stekler's study (1963), perhaps the most advanced up to that date in its discussion of alternative profitability standards, used profits before (as well as after) taxes plus interest paid in the numerator; and total assets in the denominator. No adjustment was made for current replacement cost of physical assets. (By contrast, in the methodology of this study, tangible reproducible assets have been expressed at current values; and since financial assets tend to be in current prices, a measure of profitability based on total assets expressed in current prices was used as a valid and useful measure.)

For the purposes of this review of recent literature, the profitability or rate of return measures might be grouped into four categories: 1) the "social return," or the pretax return on all incomes; 2) the total private return, a posttax concept; 3) the after-tax corporate return to equity-holders; and 4) the ratio of the market value to the replacement cost of capital — dubbed "q" in the literature.

CONCEPTS OF PROFITABILITY

Several studies, notably Stekler (1963), Nordhaus (1974) and Feldstein and Summers (1977), focus on the "social return to capital." Specifically, the latter defines the social return as corporate profits before taxes (NIPA) plus net interest, divided by the total value of the real assets of corporations in the form of fixed capital, inventories, and land. Of course, capital income, so defined, does not represent the private incentive to invest, since part of the total return is collected in taxes.

Many analysts, including Feldstein and Summers, make no adjustment for the effect of inflation on the value of corporate assets and of debt. This is because the gain to the corporation from inflation is considered as exactly offset by the loss to bondholders. The total return to capital generated by the corporation is considered as unaffected. Finally, others do not make this inflation adjustment because it is considered unnecessary, too fragile statistically, or simply unsound. (In this study, of course, those results which show the return on total assets are considered as making whatever inflation adjustment are required.)

Several studies, notably Holland and Myers (1977) and Kopcke (1978), have utilized the concept of posttax rather than pretax profitability. Since these studies were directed at examining the corporate incentive to invest, total after-tax capital income was preferred as the standard in calculating the rate of return. Because the focus is on the total return to the suppliers of capital – both debt and equity owners – no specific analysis was presumed necessary to consider inflation's impact on corporate debt in these studies. If debtors (corporations) are better off, bondholders are worse off. The net outcome is a zero sum game.

One consideration in using the posttax profits plus interest paid figures is that individual income taxes on interest paid may have an effect on the willingness of investors to supply capital. While the higher nominal interest rates which accompany inflation are reflected as higher costs to the corporation, thereby reducing the effective corporate tax rate on total capital income, they also lead to increased individual tax payments. The latter have been considered burdensome to capital investment incentives. But this has escaped serious study in the literature.

The third concept – the return to equity owners – is calculated by dividing a profit measure by the firm's net worth – the value of the firm's assets less its financial liabilities, valued at historical or market prices. At either historical or replacement cost, Shoven and Bulow (1976) and others point to the need to adjust profits for the gain equity owners experience because of an inflation-caused decline in the real value of their indebtedness.

A second general type of profitability indicator which has been much studied recently is the ratio of the market value to the replacement cost of capital, or "q." If assets are valued in the market significantly above their replacement cost, corporations will be encouraged to invest in new facilities. Contrary-wise, if assets are valued below their replacement costs, corporations which sell securities may be creating capital losses for their purchasers. In other words, when existing capital is cheap relative to new capital, q is low, and the incentive to invest is reduced. One of the virtues of q as a profitability indicator is that elaborate and perhaps incomplete inflation adjustments by statistical processes are not required. Both the calculation of the capital stocks' market value, and the determination of its replacement costs, are relatively straightforward. On the other hand, it is not easy to relate q to changes in economic policy variables.

STUDIES OF PRETAX PROFITABILITY

A central methodological step in recent analyses of trends in the pretax rate of profit, including Okun and Perry (1970), Nordhaus (1974) and Feldstein and Summers (1977) is the need for cyclical adjustment in the determination of secular trend. Feldstein-Summers attribute about all of the apparent downward trend in profitability that they found for 1970-76 to this feature. Okun-Perry also found a shortfall, after such adjustment, in the 1967-70 period. Cyclical adjustments became fashionable as "full employment budgets" began to be calculated.

Several of the analyses use the ratio of profits to GNP (rather than to assets) as the relevant measure of profitability. This approach is a close approximation to the rate of return on sales – the two would be identical except for inventory change. Since profitability varies according to the quantity of capital used in production, a change in the former would affect the results. However, if no trend in capital-output relationships can be discerned, or if it is not considered significant, the share of factor income to GNP can be used with validity in profitability measures. For short-term analysis, it is surely significant, since capital-output ratios change slowly. One advantage of the "share to GNP" approach is that the figures on income are relatively unambiguous, as compared with asset or liability valuation.

Okun-Perry

Okun and Perry (1970) experimented with the profit share of GNP in the 1950s and 1960s and found a squeeze developing in the late 1960s. This was an unexpected slowdown, even after cyclical adjustment, following a near-perfect relationship that had existed for the 1955-65 period between the profit share and economic activity. The explanation rested on a sag in productivity accompanied by a high labor compensation share. In retrospect, Okun and Perry appear perceptive in pointing to a productivity-profits nexus: the decline in profits in the 1970s has been associated with a sharp decline in the rate of growth of productivity. Their forecast of profits for 1973, however, was off the mark – on the very high side.

Nordhaus

Perhaps the most widely cited study on why profitability declined secularly was William Nordhaus' 1974 analysis, whose conclusion is stated in its title, "The Falling Share of Profits." Making many of the conceptual adjustments later officially registered in much revised form in the national accounts (IVA and CCA), he notes that profitability after 1968 declined substantially, even with inclusion of interest as part of capital income. For short run analysis, Nordhaus explains profits as the residual implied by a "normal price" equation, which relates price to normal levels of output and productivity. A mark-up over unit labor cost is the best "fit" among many trials between prices and profits in cyclical movements; but that, too, performed poorly in predicting the secular decline in profits after 1968. One explanation he offers is that businessmen perceive profits on an historical cost basis, unlike the national accounts, which includes the inventory valuation adjustment. Therefore, businessmen were confused about their costs and did not adjust their prices upwards as much as they should.

Since this price equation did not forecast well the secular decline in profits, Nordhaus turns to such variables as utilization of capacity, the capital-labor ratio (which depends on relative "rental" cost of capital and labor – the rental on capital is a function of the price of capital goods and the cost of capital) and the mark-up of price over cost to explain price and profit behavior. The analysis indicated:

– Despite sizable changes, the wage-rental ratio induced very little capital-labor substitution. As the rental of capital declined, little substitution of capital developed. This argument, of course, undercuts the power of fiscal and monetary policy to induce more capital formation.

– Price levels in this period were sufficient to cover costs, though just barely.

– The major point that emerged in the analysis was the sag in profits since 1968 resulted from a decline in the "required" rate of return. This was associated primarily with a falloff in the cost of capital, as measured by price-earnings ratios. Rates of return could fall because the cost of capital fell. Over the entire 1948-73 period, corporate capital earned an average of 7.1 percent after taxes, while the average cost of capital was 6.5 percent. After 1968, the differential was wider, averaging 1.9 percentage points. Profitability could find room to decrease, due to declining costs of capital, since it is the margin between them which is significant. Also, due to the success of aggregate demand economic policy, Nordhaus concludes that the perceived risk of capital investment could diminish, and this, too, might contribute an "equilibrium" at lower profitability rates. In addition, the tax burden has declined due to legislated reduction in rates. Thus, the combination of lower taxes and lower required rates of return on equities as risks diminished led to a decline in the before-tax cost of capital of about 55 percent from the 1948-51 period to the late 1960s. This was the precondition for lowered profitability.

In retrospect, earlier sharp capital gains in equities have been reversed and higher corporate taxes have developed due to inflation. Risk premiums probably have risen. This view is supported by Greenspan (1977), who finds that the "hurdle" rate of return on investment projects has increased. The interrelation of risk factors and profitability seems to be a fruitful field of inquiry.

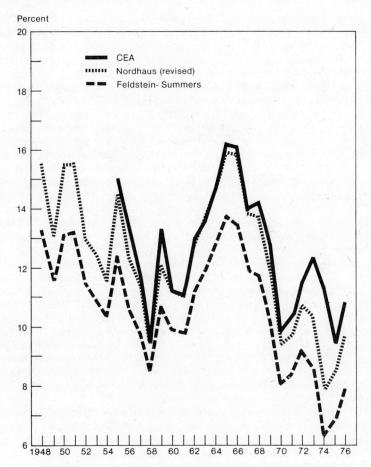

*Capital income (including interest) as percent of total physical assets at replacement cost.

Fig. 3.1. Comparison of rates of return.

Runyon (1978) has updated Nordhaus' figures, as shown in figure 3.1. The "postrevision NIPA" figures on the Nordhaus basis, after cyclical adjustment, turn out to be rather close to those calculated by Feldstein and Summers (1977). Accordingly, the difference between the Nordhaus and Feldstein-Summers estimates of the profitability trend is very limited, after the application of particular cyclical adjustments, time trends, "dummy factors" and other statistical manipulations used by Feldstein and Summers.

Feldstein and Summers

The 1977 study by Feldstein and Summers concludes that Nordhaus is incorrect with respect to evidence of a long-run downward trend in profitability. They find only very weak indications of a decline in the profit rate during the 1970s — beyond that which can be accounted for by cyclical downturns and special factors including repercussions from energy, price control, etc. The Feldstein-Summers judgment is that the cyclically adjusted "social return" on capital investment in the future will not differ significantly from the 11 percent average return on a pretax basis that has been observed over the past three decades. This would represent a high potential reward for more saving, which would provide the necessary incentive for increased capital formation (Feldstein, 1977). Thus, it is the corporate "tax wedge," plus the social security program (whose effect is to reduce private saving), and the Federal Government deficit that lowers the incentive to save.

The Feldstein-Summers methodology tests for a time trend that might explain the claimed fall in profitability (Nordhaus, 1974). The pretax rate of profit is correlated with time and various measures of utilization rates of the economy. The adjustment for cyclical swings dampens the downswing in profitability, but does not eliminate it. Indeed, raising the capacity utilization rate in manufacturing or eliminating the gap between actual and potential GNP renders the time trend statistically insignificant. Moreover, a "dummy" variable for the 1970s — a procedure by which the regression analysis gives recognition to special factors such as energy problems, price controls, etc. — shows up as statistically significant in explaining the decline in profitability in the economy during that period. Accordingly, Feldstein and Summers blame the dismal profitability record on the 1970s on transitory factors, notably the economy's adjustment to the oil price hike and wage-price controls.

The Feldstein-Summers study is the most comprehensive available statement of an optimistic view regarding future profitability. Some of the uncertainties of its conclusions and limitations need to be noted. First, the study looks only at the before-tax rate of return, when in terms of investment incentives of the corporation, the after-tax return appears more relevant. Thus, it cannot legitimately be used to support a conclusion that the "incentive to invest" has not fallen.

A second reservation regarding the Feldstein-Summers study concerns the nature of their "cyclical adjustment." They do not consider the possibility that the long-term "natural rate" of capacity utilization and potential output may have declined. If structural changes in the economy have occurred, it may no longer be possible, in the near future at least, to achieve levels of utilization achieved during the 1960s. If that were so, the Feldstein-Summers procedure overstates the appropriate cyclical adjustment. The likelihood that this, in fact, is the case is supported by the recent sharp downward trend in the rate of productivity growth and the lowered figures in both public and private estimates of potential output.

There is also some reason to believe that Feldstein and Summers, along with other investigators who have tried to cyclically adjust profits, have relied on a misspecified model of the relation between aggregate economic activity and profitability. The usual assumption is that profitability proceeds coincidentally with business cycle swings. However, profitability may depend on the rate of change rather than the level of aggregate demand. Typically, profits or profit margins peak during the recovery phase of the business cycle, rather than at its high. If this view is correct, the appropriate cyclical adjustment would be to reduce, rather than increase, the 1976 and 1977 profit rate measures. Of course, this would imply a much bleaker past performance and outlook for profit rates.

CEA Estimates

The Council of Economic Advisors in its 1978 Economic Report includes estimates of pretax rates of return on nonfinancial corporate capital. It follows Feldstein-Summers procedures, though excluding land in the denominator. Most of the recent shortfall in profitability is attributed to weakness in aggregate demand, which would support the Feldstein-Summers conclusion. "Stronger overall performance of the economy holds the promise of raising the return to capital" (1978 Economic Report, p. 69).

For convenient reference, the Nordhaus (as updated by Herbert Runyon), Feldstein-Summers, and CEA pre-tax profit series are plotted in figure 3.1. The three profit series move almost exactly in parallel. The Feldstein-Summers series is significantly lower than the other two, mainly because land is included in their calculation of the capital stock.

STUDIES OF POSTTAX PROFITABILITY

The literature on trends in the total after-tax rate of return to capital investment generally takes into account the influence of taxes on profitability, as well as the additional impact of inflation as it affects tax rates.

Separate interactions of inflation and taxation may be usefully distinguished. First, inflation raises the effective corporate profits tax rate, since taxable profits include gains resulting from understatement of replacement cost resulting from FIFO inventory accounting and depreciation of the too low historical cost of fixed assets. Second, inflation raises the value of corporate interest tax deductions, as described earlier in this study. Finally, inflation raises individual taxes on capital gains which contain both a real and inflationary component, though this has not been studied in the context of incentives to invest, in any depth.

The cumulative impact of these three factors on the effective tax rates on capital income has not been systematically addressed in the literature. Several studies – e.g., Terborgh (1976), Tideman-Tucker (1976) and Kopcke (1978) – examine only the first effect. Others (e.g., Shoven and Bulow 1975 and 1976) consider only the first two. The trend in the after-tax rate of profit in the postwar period has been carefully studied by Holland and Myers (1977), Corcoran (1977), the Council of Economic Advisors (1977, 1978 and 1979), and Kopcke (1978 and 1979).

Holland and Myers

A comprehensive study of trends in after-tax corporate profitability was undertaken by Holland and Myers (1977), who conclude that nonfinancial corporations have fared badly since the mid-1960s, but perhaps not in comparison with the 1950s. (Feldstein and Summers (1977) state in a footnote of their article (p. 213) that Holland and Myers' general conclusions "agree" with theirs on pretax profitability. That appears to be a misreading; Holland and Myers remain uncertain on trend; indeed, their statistical analysis provides a negative coefficient on time for the trend in pre-tax profits, though not much is made of this.) The cost of capital in relation to profitability is also considered and this, too, was more favorable in the mid-1960s than in the 1970s. In the last few years, the aggregate market value of nonfinancial corporations was, at most, equal to the replacement cost of their assets (a reference to "q," discussed elsewhere in this study).

Some of the results in Holland and Myers appear puzzling. An "effective tax rate" for nonfinancial corporations is shown as declining in recent years. That merely reflects the use of NIPA profits before tax plus interest paid, the latter being tax deductible. Obviously, as debt increases, the effective tax rate declines. This is misleading; it compares with a rising effective tax rate shown in table D3 of the Statistical Appendix of this study, which excludes interest paid. Indeed, applying a hypothetical tax rate to the interest part of capital income (as Holland and Myers have done in table 3.1) shows effective tax rates on total capital income as rising.

Holland and Myers experiment with regression analysis for a time trend in pretax and posttax rates of capital income during 1947-75, using the change in real GNP to measure the influence of the business cycle. The results appear inconclusive because the "t" statistic in both the pretax and posttax profitability equations is not statistically significant. Even so, the pretax coefficient on time turns out to be "negative," while the posttax coefficient is "positive."

Holland and Myers do not make much of this, but they appear concerned and uncertain of their analysis in view of their conclusion

Table 3.1. Nonfinancial Corporations:
Nominal and Effective Tax Rates
(In Percent)

Year	Statutory Tax Rate	Effective Tax Rate*	Net Interest Tax Shield**	Hypothetical All Equity Tax Rate (2) + (3)
	(1)	(2)	(3)	(4)
1946	38	58.1	1.8	59.9
1947	38	52.1	1.5	53.6
1948	38	44.2	1.3	45.5
1949	38	38.7	1.6	40.3
1950	42	55.4	1.2	56.6
1951	55.75	61.5	1.6	63.1
1952	52	56.5	2.0	58.5
1953	52	59.3	2.2	61.5
1954	52	51.7	2.8	54.5
1955	52	46.5	2.1	48.6
1956	52	46.0	2.3	48.3
1957	52	47.3	3.1	50.4
1958	52	48.5	4.3	52.8
1959	52	48.4	3.8	52.2
1960	52	46.9	4.4	51.3
1961	52	47.2	4.9	52.1
1962	52	41.7	4.7	46.4
1963	52	41.6	4.6	46.2
1964	50	38.7	4.3	43.0
1965	48	37.6	4.1	41.7
1966	48	37.5	4.5	42.0
1967	48	36.5	5.5	42.0
1968	52.8	40.9	6.5	47.4
1969	52.8	41.9	8.7	50.6
1970	49.2	39.8	12.2	52.0
1971	48	39.0	11.2	50.2
1972	48	36.8	10.1	46.9
1973	48	40.0	11.2	51.2
1974	48	48.1	15.7	63.8
1975	48	37.6	13.7	51.3
1976	48	40.2	11.2	51.4
1977	48	40.0	11.0	51.0
1978	48	42.3	11.0	53.3

*Profits tax liability divided by profits before tax (NIPA) plus net interest.
**Net interest times statutory tax rate divided by profits before tax (NIPA) plus net interest.
Source: Holland and Myers, Table 4.
Updated for 1975-78 by H.I. Liebling.

that "There is no question that NFC's have fared poorly since the mid-1960s. Whether the most recent data are viewed optimistically depends on which past period is taken as 'normal' " (p. 30).

In contrasting their conclusions with those of Nordhaus, they state first that profitability in 1946 and 1947 was not as strong as in 1948 and, thereby, find less of a decline from those years in profits over the entire postwar period. Second, as just stated, they cite the profit rates during the 1960s as being unusually high, which makes the low rates in the 1970s appear disappointing. However, Holland and Myers remain more agnostic than Feldstein and Summers regarding the likelihood that the falloff from the mid-1960s to the 1970s will be reversed.

Corcoran

According to Corcoran (1977), the rate of return for nonfinancial corporations – broadly described as a ratio of capital income (NIPA) after taxes (and adjusted for purchasing power changes of cash and trade credit) to the replacement cost of all physical and financial assets – shows the familiar pattern of peak levels in the mid-1960s and a declining movement since then. However, the values for the 1970s appear distinctly lower than in the 1950s, unlike Holland and Myers' results.

Nevertheless, Corcoran suggests that the decline in performance in these rates is not in itself damaging but must be considered together with the cost of capital. The latter is measured by capital income after taxes (NIPA) divided by the sum of market values of net corporate debt and outstanding equity. This procedure, in effect, represents a weighted measure of interest and stock yields in the denominator; and the effects of ravages of higher replacement costs of inventory and depreciation on the profits measure used in the numerator.

Ideally, the cost of capital should be indicated by the value that capital markets place on a permanent income stream of constant purchasing power. In Corcoran's formulation, however, actual earnings rather than investor's long-run expected earnings is used, since no measure of those expectations is available.

In any event, when account is taken in the numerator of the inflation's impact on profits by means of the IVA, the CCA, and an allowance for the inflation's toll on currency, demand deposits, and net trade credit, the cost of capital as defined above becomes much reduced from "standard measures." In 1976, the average adjusted cost of capital was not much different than in the 1960s, according to these estimates. By contrast, the standard conventional cost of capital measure was much higher in the 1970s than earlier.

Despite the flat performance of this new measure of cost of capital, some deterioration in the investment incentive would appear to have emerged recently. Rates of return – total capital income divided by total replacement cost of all assets – have declined. The differential between the latter and the cost of capital changed from 2.8 percent in 1965 to -1.0 percent in 1976. For 1975 and 1976, the spread had

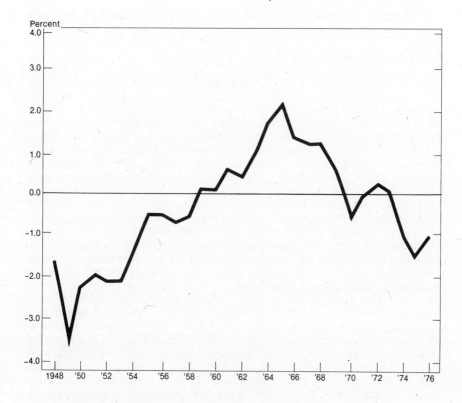

Fig. 3.2. Difference between rate of return on corporate assets
and cost of capital.

Source: Corcoran (1977).

narrowed to the smallest in over 20 years. (The annual differences between 1948 and 1976 are shown in Fig. 3.2.)

Supported by other studies, Corcoran cites a rise in the effective tax rate as a factor in the decline in lowered posttax profitability, since taxes are paid on book profits based on historical costing of depreciation and inventories. By his calculations, effective tax rates in response to inflation rose 10 percent between 1966 and 1976. This reduced the rate of return on corporate assets by 1.2 percentage points, or 2.5 percentage points after cyclical adjustment. Prior to cyclical adjustment, the rate of return declined 3.3 percentage points from 1966 to 1976.

The market value of debt and equity claims should have been and was affected by this decline. If the cost of capital remains unchanged, (e.g., at 5 percent), a one percentage point decline in rate of return would imply a 20 percent drop in replacement value of assets. Thus, the decline in "q" (analyzed below) conforms with Corcoran's analysis.

Accordingly, Corcoran suggests that the sour performance of the stock market in the past decade or so is related to inflation and the tax structure.

Kopcke

A major study of trends in profitability by Richard Kopcke of the Boston Federal Reserve Bank (1978), concluded that the after-tax return to capital has been falling steadily since 1965. It represents "neither a statistical aberration nor an entirely benign response to the recessions of the 1970s." Together with rising costs of capital (in contrast with Corcoran's flat performance) investment incentives have been undermined.

Kopcke examines the trend in profitability using two different approaches. The "trend-cycle" method involves estimating by regression an equation relating the rate of posttax profitability to cyclical indicators as the GNP gap, manufacturing capacity utilization, the unemployment rate of prime-age males, etc. However, a major contribution is that rather than choosing a year or period of years, arbitrarily, to develop a time trend for rates of return on investment as Feldstein and Summers, and other authors do for the 1970s, Kopcke searches scientifically for various possibilities of years of means of a "maximum likelihood" statistical procedure. This method establishes 1965 as a turning point in the profitability trend, a period much earlier than in Feldstein and Summers. Kopcke concludes that the normal rate of profit rose steadily from 1948 to 1965, but has declined at an annual rate of -0.07 percent since then. His statistical techniques to locate a break in the time trend represents an important contribution. (It supports the time trend analysis described subsequently in this study.)

Kopcke's second method of estimating normal rates of return involves a comparison of actual productivity with estimated "normal productivity at full capacity output." From this relation, Kopcke calculates "normal" rates of return on capital. Movements in this series parallel closely those estimated by his first method.

Note should be made of an alternative interpretation of Kopcke's estimates which appear to conform with the conclusion of Holland and Myers (1977). Figure 3.3, reproduced from Kopcke, shows the two sets of figures of the normal rate of return on capital. The inverted V pattern that shows up may be capturing not so much the decline in profitability during the 1970s, as an unusually high level of profit during the mid-1960s. The strong upwards-trend in, and levels of profits during, the 1950s might support this interpretation. Holland and Myers (1977) had concluded that "whether the most recent data are viewed optimistically or pessimistically depends on which period is taken as 'normal.' The evidence is that in the mid-1960s, NFCs' real corporate profitability was much higher, relative to the opportunity cost of capital, than it is now. On the other hand, NFCs are better off now than in the mid-1950s. Operating profitability (ROC) is the same as now but the cost of capital is lower. . ." (Holland and Myers, p. 30).

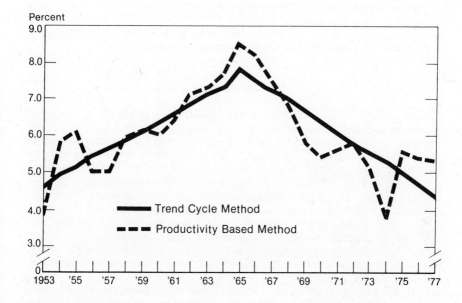

Fig. 3.3. Normal after-tax returns on capital for nonfinancial corporations.
Source: Kopcke (1977).

Presumably, Kopcke would reply that his results in recent years are
ominous because investment has been relatively insufficient for
adequate economic growth; surely so, in view of those outlays now
required for environmental and safety requirements. "Achieving national goals requires strong investment growth like that of the middle
1960s. . ." (Kopcke, p. 48).

GENERAL STUDIES OF PROFITABILITY

In the preceding review, prospective rates of return have been assumed
to be represented by returns on existing assets. Of course, in
determining the private incentive to supply capital, the investment
decision would depend on prospective rather than past returns to the
investor, whether equity – or debt-holder. Presumably, investment
would be encouraged when prospective returns exceed the cost of
capital. An approximation of prospective returns is provided in the
security markets, whose values presumably reflect a discounted flow of
expected earnings. The relation between the market value of securities
and replacement cost of assets would bear importantly on the
investment decision. The value of this relation has become known as
"q." Different sets of figures have been calculated for q.

Other general studies than on q pertain to various kinds of inflation adjustments on the income statement and balance sheet as discussed previously. They make profitability rates higher than they appear in traditional analyses. They, too, are treated in this section.

The Debate over q

Tobin's (1969) seminal article on the interactions between the real and financial sectors of the economy sets forth the basis of q: when the market value of existing physical assets is less expensive relative to their replacement costs (q is low), firms will have little incentive to invest in new capital, as against the purchase of existing capital. Conversely, when the market places a high value on existing capital (q is high), firms desiring to expand will find it cheaper to purchase new capital. The central contribution of q theory is its recognition that the incentive to invest depends on both the prospective return and the cost of holding capital. Since q incorporates both the return to future investment and its cost, many observers have come to view it as the best simple statistic for evaluating the prevailing investment climate.

Both the 1977, 1978 and 1979 Economic Reports of the CEA point to a current low level of q as an indication that investment incentives were much lower in recent years than in the second half of the 1960s. The value of q at .703 in 1978 was half of the peak reached during the 1960s, when business fixed investment was about 10.5 percent of real GNP, as compared with 10.0 percent in the mid-1970s. Both Economic Reports ascribe the decline in q to unfavorable expectations shared by business managers and investors in equities. These expectations presumably were related to economic policies which were viewed unfavorably in the securities markets, lowered prospects of profitability, and uncertainties regarding inflation. The decline in q might also have been affected by energy factors, which lowered the value of existing equipment, and the uncertainty created by government regulations.

All q series, in addition to those presented in the CEA Economic Reports, indicate a rapid decline in the figures over the last decade. Moreover, cyclical adjustment is not a real issue in the interpretation of q because the market's long-term expectations presumably have been incorporated in the levels. Nevertheless, there are some qualifications to these measures. The most important of these is the distinction between values of marginal and average q. The market value of existing capital may be reduced by many extraneous or exogenous factors, such as a change in technology, which would render existing capital costly to use or obsolete. Yet, such events may raise the return on marginal new investment. For example, due to the oil price hike, the market value of some existing energy-producing capital was reduced; at the same time, this raised the incentive to invest in new energy-conserving equipment and structures.

Aside from these conceptual points, there are measurement problems in the calculation of q. The most serious flaws in the calculations, such as those found in the CEA Economic Reports, Holland and Myers

(1977), and Ciccolo (1975), result from the calculation of the denominator – the replacement cost of corporate assets. In principle, this should reflect the value of all corporate assets and liabilities. Yet the value of land, patents, many monopoly rents, financial holdings, and pension liabilities are usually excluded. Since these components, particularly the last one, are quite volatile and could easily have changed relative to the value of physical capital over the past decade, it is difficult to conclude whether movements in q are, in fact, reflections of changes in profit expectations or in the value of corporate assets, properly defined to include those above aforementioned elements.

The Rate of Return to Equity Holders

Some studies have focused on the return to equity-holders as the principal criterion of the earning power of corporations. Perhaps the principal issue that is addressed concerns the "distortion" of profit figures resulting from inflation, particularly the real value of corporate indebtedness, which is said to be a gain properly added to profits. This issue has been considered in detail by Shoven and Bulow (1976), Malkiel and von Furstenberg (1977) and Cagan and Lipsey (1978).

The most comprehensive recent study of the effect of inflation on the rate of return on equity capital may be found in Cagan and Lipsey (1978). They make four adjustments which affect profits, profit rates and q:

1) standard NIPA adjustments of IVA and CCA for costs of using up of fixed assets and inventories, 2) changes in the market price of financial assets and liabilities, (e.g., as interest rates rise, dollar values of debt diminish and net worth increases.) 3) capital gains or losses on tangible assets, and 4) changes in the real value of net financial liabilities for changes in the price level.

The effects of these adjustments on profits after tax is shown in table 3.2. Since inflation reduces the real value of financial assets and liabilities and since nonfinancial corporations are net debtors, a profit gain is presumed to have developed in real terms from depreciation in the purchasing power of net liabilities.

Two inflation impacts on debt have been differentiated in Cagan and Lipsey. In addition to the reduction in real indebtedness due to price level increases, Cagan and Lipsey introduce a gain to profits resulting from higher interest rates which may accompany inflation. Whether realized or not, it is argued that a capital gain accrues to a firm if the market value of its outstanding debt declines, since the firm has the option of buying back its debt. "If this benefit is recorded as a one-time capital gain in the dollar price of the bond at the time the price fell, subsequent yearly increases in the dollar price as it rises to its par redemption value are recorded as capital losses. . . . After these adjustments, profits are increased initially by the capital gain when interest rates rise and are not affected thereafter; there occurs no

Table 3.2. Nonfarm Nonfinancial Corporations
Profits Including and Excluding Adjustments for the Effects of Inflation
(Billions of 1964 Dollars)

	After-tax Profits Conventional Basis (1)	Inventory Valuation Adjustment (2)	Capital Consumption Adjustment (3)	After-tax Profits, National Accounts Basis (4)	Change in Market Value of Net Financial Liabilities (5)	Real Capital Gains (+) or Losses (-) on Land (6)	Reproducible Tangible Assets (7)	Change in Dollar Price of Debt Outstanding at Beginning of Year (8)	Profits Adjusted for Change in Real Value of Net Financial Liabilities, and Market Value of Long-Term Debt (4) - (5) + (6) + (7) - (8) (9)
1955	26.5	-2.0	-2.4	22.1	-0.2	4.0	6.9	-1.7	34.9
1960	22.4	0.3	-2.4	20.3	-0.9	2.2	-1.6	+2.4	19.4
1965	38.3	-1.9	3.5	39.9	-2.1	4.1	2.7	-2.5	51.3
1970	23.6	-4.1	1.3	20.8	-7.1	1.9	11.8	+16.2	25.4
1971	27.0	-3.8	0.4	23.6	-5.3	4.7	8.9	+19.1	23.4
1972	32.7	-4.9	2.0	29.8	-6.4	8.1	11.0	+2.2	53.1
1973	39.6	-13.0	1.3	27.9	-17.4	9.9	31.8	-16.0	103.0
1974	40.9	-25.4	-1.9	13.6	-23.9	2.9	41.5	-25.0	106.9
1975	37.3	-6.9	-6.9	23.5	-13.6	3.7	15.0	+20.6	35.2
1976	44.2	-7.7	-7.9	28.6	-9.7	1.3	-1.0	+34.3	4.3
1977	46.3	-7.4	-8.7	30.2	-19.8	1.4	29.9	-11.0	92.3

Source: Cagan and Lipsey (1978), table 2.

double counting of the contribution to profits of lower interest rates" (Cagan and Lipsey, p. 16).

Table 3.3 presents Cagan and Lipsey's estimates of profits, showing the effects of various adjustments for selected years. All the figures are in 1964 dollars to provide comparability. The results show very clearly the importance of the inflation adjustment to net indebtedness. In 1977, for example, after-tax profits on a conventional basis were $46.3 billion. The adjustments involving valuing capital consumption allowances and inventories at replacement rather than historic costs reduce this figure to about $30 billion. However, the adjustment for inflation and rising interest rates, which moves in the opposite direction, dwarfs these adjustments. The effect of inflation on nominal liabilities, shown in column (5) is more than sufficient to offset the replacement cost adjustments. The reduction of the market value of debt due to higher interest rates also has significant impact. The final figure (shown in column (9) is $92.3 billion, almost 130 percent greater than NIPA profits. This pattern is not uncommon. In 1974, for example, NIPA profits were only $13.6 billion, while "fully-adjusted profits" were $106.9 billion.

Cagan and Lipsey build upon the earlier study of Shoven and Bulow (1976), who treat repercussions of inflation and rate increases on debt as forms of income to corporations in line with an accrual concept of accounting. These adjustments were made subsequently by Cagan and Lipsey. Shoven and Bulow (1976) pose two different income concepts, a Haig-Simon accrual and a Pigou-Marshall capital-maintenance concept. Basically, the issue of difference is accrued versus realized gains to income. The former is favored by Shoven and Bulow. The purchasing-power-accrual concept of corporate income requires recording of all assets and liabilities at their market values to determine changes in net worth. Capital gains would be recorded in the income statement, whether realized or not, when inflation diminishes the value of debt. Real depreciation of net financial liabilities due to general inflation is a second major adjustment.

Adjusted profits after tax, as percent of net worth, appear not unusually low, as Feldstein and Summers found, except by comparison with the mid-1960s. Indeed, they appear slightly higher in the 1970s on average than in the 1950s. (See Statistical Appendix, Table D12.)

Malkiel

In light of the correction of profits for real capital gains on debt, the key question of the stock market's poor performance in recent years becomes puzzling. Malkiel (1977) concludes that the market is very much undervaluing future returns, and so forecasts significant increases over the next few years. He bases this calculation, in part, on the declining real value of corporate indebtedness and, in part, on the Feldstein and Summers conclusion that the rate of profit is only temporarily depressed.

While his forecast is certainly plausible, it does not consider three important mitigating factors. First, the presumed gains from inflation that corporations have been experiencing on their debt will decline, as more of it is replaced by new issues at higher interest rates which reflect prevailing rates of inflation. In any event, Malkiel does not take account of the extremely rapid growth in unfunded corporate liabilities, as described in Chapter 2. Third, in relying on the Feldstein and Summers analysis of an uptilt in profitability consequent to cyclical recovery, Malkiel confuses the role of pre- and posttax profits. It is the posttax rate of profit, not considered by Feldstein and Summers, which is relevant to equity owners. As continued inflation causes book profits to become overstated, effective tax rates will rise so that the posttax rate of profit will fall even if the pretax rate remains constant. On balance, a relatively agnostic posture regarding future movements in the level of the stock market, and in q, seems most appropriate.

4 A Refutation of the Feldstein and Summers Results Showing No Decline in Pretax Profitability

Because it has attracted so much attention and provided a fecund methodological approach adopted by many in subsequent studies, a special analysis of the Feldstein and Summers approach is merited, even though it was briefly reviewed earlier in this report. Indeed, the principal support in recent years for the contention that profitability remains favorable on a secular basis rests on the analysis provided by Feldstein and Summers in 1977. Directed towards the trend in the "total return to capital," Feldstein and Summers apply their attention to profits before tax (NIPA) plus net interest paid. Prior to a special cyclical adjustment, the data show that pretax total or capital income as a percent of net stock of physical capital at replacement cost has declined in recent years.

They define the rate of return as:

π_t^n = net profits of nonfinancial corporations in year t
INT_t = total net interest paid by these corporations in year t
K_t^n = the value of the net fixed capital stock at the end of year t
INV_t = the value of inventories at the end of year t
L_t = the value of land at the end of year t.

All of these values are measured in current prices.

The 1948-76 average for nonfinancial corporations was 10.6 percent in the original calculations. Higher rates had prevailed for two earlier decades, averaging about 11 and 12 percent in the 1950s and the 1960s. However, for the overlapping decade of 1966-75, the rate of return was only 9.5 percent; moreover, the 1970-76 rate was 7.9 percent — far below the long-term average.

Nevertheless, Feldstein and Summers conclude that their analysis

Table 4.1. Annual Rate of Return on Nonfinancial
Corporate Capital*

Average	Actual	Cyclically Adjusted
	(percent)	
1948-76	10.6	11.2
1948-69	11.5	11.8
1960-69	11.7	12.1
1970-76	7.9	9.2
1976	7.9	10.3

*Capital income as percent of net stock of physical assets at replacement cost.

indicates no secular decline in profitability and, indeed, that the 1970s represents merely a temporary fall to unusually low profitability. That analysis depended heavily on a cyclical adjustment which raises the pretax rate of return substantially, as shown in table 4.1, the original Feldstein and Summers calculation.

Nevertheless, the above data do not clearly support a view that the economy, had it operated at close to "full employment," did indicate a fall in profitability in the 1970s. The cyclically adjusted rate of return for 1970-76 was 9.2 percent – clearly below the 1948-76 average of 11.2 percent and significantly below the 1960s average of 12.2 percent. In 1976, the original Feldstein and Summers' cyclically adjusted return was 10.3 percent.

However, the uncertain effect of this cyclical adjustment is illustrated by the decline in 1977 to a calculated 9.8 percent, as shown in Table D1b of the Statistical Appendix. The second column of that table represents an update by the author of the original calculations. This still appears low by conventional standards, even though capital income rose 13 percent in 1977.

The cyclical adjustment is numerically derived by a coefficient from a regression equation which shows the effect on profitability resulting from changes in the gap between the official estimates of actual and potential GNP. According to Feldstein and Summers, a one percent change in the gap was associated with a one-third percent change in the rate of profitability. At first glance, this concept appears acceptable on the basis that the rate of utilization of capacity in the economy induce lower or higher total costs per unit of output, as overhead expenses are spread.

Nevertheless, this gap, when used as a cyclical adjustment factor, is deficient in several respects:

-   The nonfinancial corporate product is less than three-fifths of total GNP. Accordingly, it needs to be established that using so large a proxy for nonfinancial corporations as total GNP yields unbiased estimates.

- Even if GNP gaps were to be used as a basis for cyclical adjustment, a choice of several gaps has become available recently. To begin with, the official CEA estimates of potential GNP, upon which the gap is calculated, has been revised downward since the Feldstein and Summers analysis was done. Using the revised figures, the value of the cyclical correction is lowered. Moreover, the Federal Reserve Bank of St. Louis has calculated GNP growths at so-called full employment and so have Professors Perloff and Wachter of the University of Pennsylvania. The several measures of gaps fluctuate in roughly similar fashion, though distinct differences in amplitude clearly exist, as shown in Fig. 1.1.

- Had the St. Louis GNP gap been used as an adjustment factor, profitability would have been raised only 1.7 percent, as compared with 2.2 percent with the use of the CEA gap factor. Profitability would then be viewed as relatively low in 1976. Using the Perloff-Wachter gap, the adjustment in profitability would have been even less-nearly .5 percent lower than that of the St. Louis gap.

- The Feldstein and Summers' analysis assumes that some desirably high utilization rate in the economy, conceived in terms of closing the GNP gap, is the proper test of the trend in profitability. The actual performance of real GNP growth, calculated on some trend basis, could well be a better guide. "Normal" profits – rather than some conceived optimal profit rate which develops only at infrequent intervals of full employment – is a rational alternative criterion.

- The currently low level of capacity utilization may not be temporary. Aside from the difficulties of measuring "full employment GNP," a considerable period of time may elapse before complications are resolved concerning energy, inflation effects, new social attitudes affecting productivity, unemployment rates, etc. An early return, short of several years and perhaps longer, to CEA GNP potential growth rates, even as recently redefined, might appear less probable than at first assumed.

FELDSTEIN AND SUMMERS AND TIME TRENDS

The conclusion drawn by Feldstein and Summers on the absence of change in the trend of profitability revealed by "time" is stated continuously. Though the value of the trend is regarded as not statistically different from zero, they remain concerned that the regression shows a rate of return that would fall by one-eighth of its value in a decade. Variables on the utilization rate of the economy do meet tests of statistical significance, while the tests for a Feldstein-

Summers time trend do not. Nevertheless, the sign of the "time" variable remains negative in each of the eight equations presented in their analysis. Indeed, the value of the time variable increased in several of the equations when the "pressure of the economy" variables were added, as compared with using "time" alone as an independent variable. It is this which led them to use the "dummy procedure" for the 1970s as an alternative to explain low profitabilities in that period. Problems related to energy, wage-price controls and unprecedented inflation are said to have exercised special depressing effects on profitability.

But, a close reading of their work shows their misgivings by the following: "The conventional interpretation of the standard errors implies that these coefficients differ from zero in a marginally significant way" (emphasis added). Indeed the "t" statistic, which ordinarily would require a value of 2 or more with these data to register statistical significance, is only 1.6. One sentence past this statement, they draw the conclusion that, "the evidence thus indicates that 1970-76 has generally been a period of unusually low rates of return. . ." (p. 222).

The experimental use of so-called dummy variables for other time periods than the 1970s that might have yielded more significant results in determining a time trend is not noted. Chapter 5 provided a discussion of the application of the "dummy" procedure to such other time periods. That analysis shows that the 1970s do not necessarily represent a period that yields the most statistically significant results. Greater experimentation in choice of time periods by Feldstein and Summers would have been desirable.

Finally, the tests of statistical significance – which Feldstein and Summers indicate show no trend for time – may be interpreted differently. They are aware that even with a low "t" statistic, the coefficient for time, nevertheless, is large. Hence, they worry about it – and they should. The basic factor contributing to the low value of the "t" statistic (the value of the coefficient in relation to its standard error) is the large standard error of estimate of the time coefficient. It makes a difference in the interpretation of the "t" statistic if the relevant numbers are (a) -0.13 divided by 0.14, indicating no statistical significance, instead of (b) -.0060 divided by .0064. Both have a "t" value of 0.94, which carries no statistical significance. But (a) would worry an analyst more than (b). It is supportive of this interpretation that all of Feldstien and Summers' equations have negative time coefficients that appear worrisome.

5 The Results of the Statistical Analysis: Declines in Secular Profitability

A great number of statistical experiments which bear on the trend of profitability were performed in the course of this study. They are not all specifically analyzed, but they are reported in the tables shown in the Statistical Appendix.

The overall conclusion that emerges is that relatively low rates of profitability in the 1970s have developed for nonfinancial corporations, even after allowance has been made for cyclical influences. The major statistics bearing on this finding have been collected in the figures and tables that have been shown in Chapter 1.

In general, the regression analyses show that after allowance for cyclical influences and for time trend:

- Rates of return on tangible capital or total assets and on net worth have decreased in the 1970s. A comprehensive set of tables bearing on these matters is presented in the Statistical Appendix.

- Profit margins, as developed from factor shares of GNP, also have trended down over this period. Mainly, this has resulted from a rising share of labor compensation.

These results point to a "structural" change affecting profitability in the U.S. economy. The period since the mid-1960s has differed in such fashion that its model contains elements which generate a lower "normal" rate of profit than earlier. Many experiments with complex econometric procedures were used to test this hypothesis. Tentatively, that hypothesis is supported in the tables of the Statistical Appendix.

Before proceeding to the results of these experiments, it may be useful to recapitulate the breadth of choice in the measures of profitability as the dependent variable in the statistical analyses. They would include profits before or after taxes; profits before taxes plus interest (as a measure of the "social return" from capital); profits after taxes plus interest (as a measure of the private return); "gross profits," which are inclusive of depreciation; so-called "cash flow," which represents retained earnings plus depreciation, etc.

The many variations just indicated represent only the numerator in determining trends of profitability. The denominator also may be conceived as total assets, either in historical or replacement cost, nonfinancial assets, tangible assets, or other combinations or selections from compilations of balance sheet figures for nonfinancial corporations.

Another set of concepts that might enter into the denominator relates to production or sales figures as represented by gross nonfinancial corporate product; or "final sales" (GNP less change in inventory). As noted earlier, corporate profit, as a percent of output or sales – a so-called "profit margin" – is an essential element in comprehension of pricing policies that eventually links with the trend in profitability.

However, this study has concluded from its statistical analyses that most measures of profitability of nonfinancial corporations show a downtrend in the 1970s that registers more than cyclical influence. The choice of the profitability variable was not crucial in establishing this finding. Furthermore, the experiments conducted with profits and other property income (or labor compensation, its complement) supported this view in a specially compelling fashion.

PROFIT MARGINS AND PROFITS

Trends in profitability, or profit "squeezes" or "excesses" are frequently viewed in terms of the share of corporate profits to GNP (e.g., Okun and Perry, 1970). Indeed, this share does fluctuate more widely than most other returns to the factors of production in response to business cycle changes. After all, profits represent a residual, that which is left after the more sluggish reaction of changes in labor compensation and other costs to scale of operations. In other words, as a share of product, total costs fluctuate less than revenues in business cycle swings. For this reason (and several others noted below), an analysis of the secular trend in profitability is made particularly difficult.

Because profits and profitability is so difficult to define, an analysis of the labor compensation share of GNP over time may yield a better indication of trend in profitability than one devoted directly to the property share. Estimates of the value of labor compensation are less difficult. Pertaining to property income, the problems in the measurement of depreciation are well-known – indeed, that issue has not finally been settled by the now officially accepted convention of straight-line depreciation in the NIPA concepts. Indeed, as Terborgh (1976) has emphasized again, the decision would well be reconsidered.

Furthermore, looking at the labor compensation rather than the capital income share avoids, to a degree, the issue of changing roles of debt and equity financing. Shifts in that role may not affect analysis of the return to a factor of production in the short- and perhaps interim-run. Aside from tax benefits, interest payments represent a cost to be

Table 5.1. Shares of Profits Before Tax (NIPA) and Labor Compensation
of Gross Product, Nonfinancial Corporations
(percent)

	Profits Plus	Compensation	
Averages:	Net Interest	Of Employees	Other*
1948-78	15.6	65.1	19.2
1950-59	16.9	64.8	18.3
1960-69	16.4	64.3	19.4
1948-69	16.8	64.5	18.7
1970-79	12.8	66.7	20.5

*Capital Consumption Allowance with capital consumption adjustment plus indirect taxes, plus transfers less subsidies.

considered in the investment decision; if they rise, their impact may be as important as higher costs from any source.

With respect to the share of labor compensation to gross product, the message is startlingly clear: it has risen sharply over time – as shown in table 5.1. That share averaged 64.3 percent in 1960-69, as compared with 66.7 percent in the 1970s.

Of course, it has been observed that the high levels of profitability in the 1960s makes the 1970s look low; the 1970s are said to be in line with the 1950s. But, if the compensation of employees share is used as a touchstone, the 1970s would not support that theory – the share was higher in the 1970s than in the 1950s, though not by much. If the Korean War years of 1950-53 are excluded, the share in the 1950s was as low as 65.2 percent. (The pattern remains similar when percentages of labor compensation to product are compared on a value added basis, i.e., net of indirect taxes and payments less subsidies, etc. Table 5.2 shows annual figures and averages over several periods of time.

RATES OF RETURN ON ASSETS

The available measures of profits on capital income in relation to depreciable assets, total assets, or net worth typically show smaller values for the 1970s than for the mid-1960s. The controversial inflation-adjusted figures by Cagan and Lipsey (1978) do not follow this pattern.

Cyclical adjustments or analysis of time trends have been undertaken to explain the low values for the 1970s reported in many studies. These are particularly complicated processes when addressed by econometric methods and deserve special attention. This study's econometric analysis tends to support a view of low profitability in the 1970s, after both cyclical adjustment and time trend analysis.

Table 5.2. Annual Rate of Return, Nonfinancial Corporations

	Pre-Tax Capital Income Return on Tangible Capital			After-Tax Return on Net Worth		
	Feldstein-Summers[a]	CEA[b]	Holland-Myers[c]	CEA[b]	Kopcke[c,d]	Cagan-Lipsey[b]
			(percent)			
1948-77	10.6	12.4	6.8	6.1	15.7	8.3
1950-59	11.1	n.a.	5.9	n.a.	n.a.	n.a.
1960-69	11.7	13.7	8.0	6.5	n.a.	8.7
1948-69	11.5	13.2	7.1	6.1	n.a.	9.0
1970-77	7.9	10.8	5.6	6.2	11.9	8.1

a) Final year is 1976.   b) Initial year is 1955.
c) Final year is 1975.   d) Initial year is 1965.
n.a. – Not available.

THE DILEMMA OF THE CYCLICAL ADJUSTMENT

While some analyses of secular trend consider "averages" of some sort in simple or complex ways, others have sought to find "full employment" values for profitability in order to neutralize the effects of business cycles. Typically, this procedure has involved regression analysis to develop a coefficient value for cyclical influences. This is used to raise the profit share, or, more typically, the profit rate to a full employment level. A regression coefficient value for the so-called GNP "gap" has been commonly used for this purpose.

This study has utilized new measures of "pressure" variables to eliminate cyclical influences. In effect, they represent variations in the operating rates of the economy. The gap can be variously estimated, because both official and private measures of potential GNP growth have been developed. They are shown in the fig. 1.1. Indeed, the Council of Economic Advisors (CEA) in 1978 provided a new series of potential GNP growth, lowering the estimates for earlier years considerably; for example, it resulted in halving of the 1977 GNP gap from the one previously available. These estimates were reduced further in CEA's 1979 Economic Report, too late to include in the regression analysis of rates of return that is shown in the Statistical Appendix. Perloff and Wachter (1978) have developed a series which reduces this gap again by an additional half. Another new series for the gap has been provided by Rasche and Tatom (1977) of the Federal reserve Bank of St. Louis.

Most full employment output series have been constructed by fitting trends to actual output and, therefore, are strongly influenced by cyclical peaks. Values for potential GNP as calculated previously usually were consistently below potential, except for 1965-1969. By contrast, the Perloff-Wachter series is based on a so-called production function involving three factor inputs – labor, capital and energy– and is subject to the constraint of nonaccelerating inflation. The estimates show that by the fourth quarter of 1977 the economy was at full employment. A similar pattern is exhibited by the potential GNP figures developed at the Federal Reserve Bank of St. Louis.

Cyclically adjusted profitability rates vary considerably when the several GNP gaps are used for adjustment. The profitability rate for capital income (profits before tax plus interest) shows that use of the Perloff-Wachter gap fixes the profit rate for 1970-77 at 9.49 percent. This compares with 7.99 percent as an "actual" for this period. A striking aspect of the new cyclically adjusted figures is the sharp reduction in 1970-77, from the cyclically adjusted rates of former decades (see table D1b in the Statistical Appendix).

A still further refinement is a cyclical adjustment for trend growth of GNP, rather than by means of GNP gaps. Charlotte Boshan and Walter Ebank of the National Bureau of Economic Research have calculated this growth rate in a recent paper (1978). Application of this growth rate as a cyclical factor shows that rates of return for nonfinancial corporations in 1970-77 were virtually equal to the "actuals" (see table D1B). That is a result which aught to weight heavily in evaluating current profitability.

THE RESULTS OF THE REGRESSION ANALYSIS

The trends in profitability on which regression experiments were made centered on eight definitions of profitability – though many more seemed applicable and in fact were attempted. (Not all the results are shown in the Statistical Appendix. Among them were such variables as "the sum of" retained earnings plus depreciation; profits after tax plus depreciation; etc.) In the regressions shown in the Statistical Appendix, the dependent variable consisted of a profit rate of nonfinancial corporations expressed as a percentage. The rate was calculated from a:

- Numerator of profits before and after tax, either on a straight-line or double declining balance with respect to depreciation (as well as with IVA); and with and without the inclusion of net interest paid.

- Denominator which remained the same in all cases, consisting of both nonresidential and residential depreciable capital (including inventories). These were estimates of the Commerce Department (Musgrave, 1976 and updated), which were centered at midyear. It might be stressed again that the choice of the denominator was not crucial with respect to the experiments. Fig. 1.8 depicts the nearly identical   level and movement of the rate of return on depreciable assets and on net worth.

The analysis in the form of regressions proceeded along two basic lines:

- Those which relied completely upon a time trend and alternative "pressure variables" to show the degree of utilization of the economy. The "pressures" represented the several available measures of utilization rates of manufacturing capacity and of GNP gaps.

- Those which sought to reflect the special influences prevailing in certain years – e.g., energy or other factors – by the use of dummy variables.

THE FIRST TRIALS

With respect to the first set of regression, it became evident that profitability depended upon the degree of utilization of the economy. The spreading of fixed costs over a large volume of output always exerted a powerful effect on profitability. In terms of R2 (the coefficient of determination), the range registered was between 60 and 90 percent. Profits before tax as a rate of return over depreciable assets scored among the highest in R2 (see Statistical Appendix).

Many, but not all, of the regression results relating profitability to time alone, as the sole independent variable, showed no statistically significant time trend in the period 1950-77. However, as Feldstein and Summers (1977) had noted (and been concerned about), all but one measure of profitability registered a negative value for the time trend. This appeared to indicate some general tendency, even though many of the tests, per se, showed little statistical significance. (In other words, the "t" statistic was not significant at the 95 percent level.)

Nevertheless, the uniformity of results regarding the negative value of the time variable possesses significance. (Table D11 in the Statistical Appendix gathers together the "time" coefficients of all of the regressions.)

The Results with Pressure Variables

When pretax rates of return were regressed against a "pressure" variable and time, the time coefficients turned statistically significant. This occurred in three cases, in connection with the following "pressure" variables"

- The Federal Reserve capacity utilization rate ("t" value of 2.18).
- The St. Louis GNP ("t" value of 3.56).
- The Wharton Capacity utilization rate ("t" value of 2.11).
  (Note: "t" values of about 2 or more are considered to register statistical significance.)

The tests of significance indicated indeterminate results for corporations on a posttax basis. This was an outcome that was difficult to interpret. Perhaps the size of the profit rate measure affected the results. Estimates of profits before tax averaged 10.72 percent during 1948-77, while profits after tax earned 5.26 percent. A change of one percent from a high rate of return, as in pretax profits, represents a less serious matter than a similar fall from the lower posttax rate of return. Table 5.3 shows weighting of the time coefficients by these relative rates of return.

Table 5.3. Weighted Coefficients for "Time"*

	None	CEA gap	STL gap	FR UCAP	WM UCAP	Q gap
Profits after tax	-.017	-.008	-.013	-.014	-.019	-.027
Profits before tax	-.020	-.011	-.018	-.018	-.023	-.021
Profits after tax + interest	.001	.007	.004	-.003	-.001	-.007
Profits before tax + interest	-.010	-.003	-.008	-.008	-.012	-.011

*Based on regressions for 1950-1977. (See table A in Statistical Appendix for glossary of terms.) Source: From regression equations utilizing indicated pressure variable.

The larger value of the negative time trend in the pretax profitability figures, as compared with posttax, suggests the omission of a variable. The values for R^2 were higher in the pretax profit equation, especially when interest paid was included. These findings might have been expected since net interest has increased rapidly since 1965, reducing the statistical significance of the downtrend in profit rates. As previously noted, the inclusion of net interest may be justified on a pretax basis, as being a part of the social return on investment. There is less justification for including interest on a posttax basis as part of a "social return" concept, since the posttax measure presumably represents profitability after allowing all "costs," including interest costs. (However, other studies by Nordhaus, Kopcke, and Holland and Myers do depend upon profits after tax plus interest as the relevant profit variable.)

Dummy Variables: Appropriate for the 1960s or 1970s?

Another set of trials strongly suggest that the experience of the 1960s does not sway the judgment that a downward trend in the rate of profitability developed in the 1970s. Feldstein and Summers make the case for special circumstances in the 1970s as a reason for using "dummies" for that period – a procedure explained below. The "t" values were found to be marginally statistically significant. However, the effect of using the dummy procedure was to change the value for the time trend into a statistically insignificant number. Hence, they concluded no secular downward fall in profitability.

Others argue a different case: special circumstances for the mid-1960s. The latter included a low rate of inflation, relatively high productivity, relatively low unit labor costs, and a high capacity utilization rate – conditions especially beneficial to high profit rates. This assumes that the mid-1960s were unusual and, therefore, should not be used as a standard of attainment from which a downtrend in profitability would be registered. And, indeed, such a period in the mid-1960s might hardly be considered as representative by current standards; it might be considered as outside the normal range of experience that might develop. The issue becomes: which is less representative, the 1970s or the mid-1960s? If it were the mid-1960s, then a downdrift in profitability surely has occurred. But it might be considered a downdrift to "normal" profit rates.

The statistical procedure that gives weight to special circumstances, without losing the contribution of other influencing factors, is the dummy device. This study applies this standard econometric method to the experience of the last 30 years in determining the trend in profitability. Special weight was given to 1962-68 in view of apparently high rates of return during those years. Using capital income (NIPA profits before tax plus interest) as the dependent variable, the coefficient of the dummy when using the CEA gap and "time" as the other independent variables was 2.5, indicating that the rate of return averaged 2.5 percent above the experience of the other years since 1950. In the case of the St. Louis gap as the alternative independent "pressure" variable, the coefficient for the dummy was 1.7, indicating that the rate of return averaged 1.7 percent above normal experience. (In the Statistical Appendix, the 1962-68 dummy is designated as D60 in the several tables.)

In each case, the dummy-affected results still leave the rate of return values for 1962-68 high relative to the actual values. The general conclusion might be drawn that the dummies are reflecting special influence; but even after that allowance, an underlying fall in profitability since then may be discerned when the perspective encompasses the entire period of the 30 years in review.

A comparison of the equations, with and without dummies, shows a larger number of "t" values above 2 for the time variable in the dummied approach. The significance of this rests on the apparent circumstance that the mid-1960s were affected by special circumstances at least as much, if not more than those cited for the 1970s, as Feldstein and Summers do. Thus, the 1970s need not be considered as specially affected years – at least not more so than other periods. Indeed, the evidence for a statistically significant negative time trend becomes fairly impressive with the use of a dummy variable for 1962-68, as shown in table 5.4.

Table 5.4. Values for "t" on Time Variable*

	Capital Income	Profits Before Taxes (NIPA)	Profits After Taxes (NIPA)
Pressure Variable CEA gap			
Dummied	2.667	2.718	4.830
No Dummy	.377	1.186	.431
Pressure Variable STL gap			
Dummied	4.730	3.479	7.859
No Dummy	2.159	3.561	.927

*Values for "t" on time variable with indicated cyclical pressure measure as second independent variable.

THE INFLATION-ADJUSTED RATE OF RETURN

Another standard measure is the corporate after-tax (NIPA) return on stockholders' equity.

Two approaches to implement this concept are possible: If interest income is excluded from the numerator, then the denominator of a stockholder's net worth should measure tangible assets less net financial liabilities. A second approach is the standard measure of profits after tax (NIPA) as percent of net worth.

With respect to the latter set of figures, over the past 30 years there would appear to be little difference in trend than has been indicated by the foregoing analysis. The figures in table 5.5 clearly show some fall off for the 1970s, just as the other profit measures do.

Table 5.5. Nonfinancial Corporations:
Profits After Tax (NIPA)
as Percent of Depreciable Assets and Stockholders' Equity*

	Depreciable Assets	Stockholders' Equity
1969-78	5.3	5.1
1950-59	5.3	4.8
1960-69	6.6	6.4
1970-78	3.3	3.6

*Physical assets at replacement cost.
Source: See table D6 in Statistical Appendix.

However, inflation is a factor that may need to be considered. The real value of a firm's financial liabilities is said to decline as prices rise. This decline has been considered a gain for shareholders that must be added to profit. (As noted previously, this adjustment may not consider properly the corporation's increased liabilities with respect to pension funds). The following figures illustrate the effect of a 10 percent general price rise on outstanding debt:

	Before	After
Assets	$1,000,000	$1,100,000
Debt	300,000	300,000
Net Worth	$700,000	800,000

The real value of net worth need have risen only by $70,000; the additional $30,000 might be considered a capital gain.

Two measures of return on stockholders' equity, as calculated by the Council of Economic Advisors, adjusts for inflation. They do not appear to alter the pattern of change described earlier, as shown in table 5.6.

Table 5.6. Inflation-Adjusted After-Tax Return
On Stockholders' Equity
(percent)

	Published[1]	
	1978 Estimates	1979 Estimates
1955-59	5.2	4.9
1960-69	6.5	6.9
1970-77	5.6*	5.8
1976	5.8	4.8
1977	5.9	6.2
1978	n.a.	8.9

*Excluding 1974.
[1]Corrected for inflation effect by change in manufacturers' prices.

COST OF CAPITAL AND PROFITABILITY

Though the rate of profitability may decline, little damage may be wrought on the rate of investment if the cost of capital falls to the same or greater extent. (Estimates of the cost of capital vary considerably. However, Nordhaus (1974) noted that the complex measures of the cost of capital performed little differently than such a simple measure as an uncorrected Standard & Poor's earnings-price ratio. Indeed, his major point is that while profits do represent a declining share of GNP, that did not have such serious implications because the cost of capital also has fallen.)

As figure 5.1 shows, however, the cost of capital, which had remained fairly flat during the 1960s, turned up sharply in 1971. (This measure of the cost of capital represents a weighted average of the equity and after-tax debt shares of total financing, as developed but unpublished by Dr. Gary Wenglowski of Goldman, Sachs and Co. In 1978, the equity share weight was 40 percent of this total.)

As can be observed from table 5.7, the differential between the cost of capital and the rate of return on a profits after-tax basis had

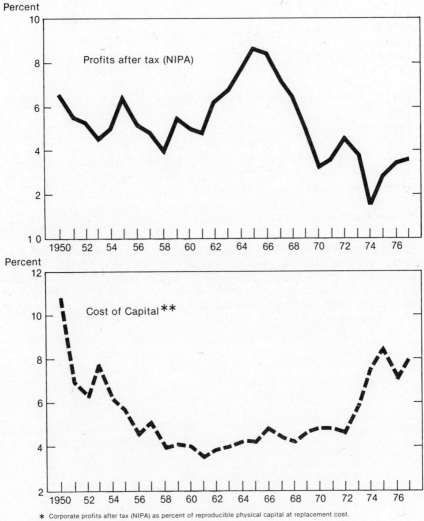

* Corporate profits after tax (NIPA) as percent of reproducible physical capital at replacement cost.

** Weighted average of price-earnings ratio and corporate after-tax bond yield.

Fig. 5.1. After tax profit rates on nonfinancial corporate capital compared to the cost of capital.

Table 5.7. Cost of Capital and Profit Rates
(in percent)

Averages	Cost of Capital (1)	Capital Income (2)	Profits After Tax (NIPA) (3)	Differences (2) - (1)	(3) - (1)
1949-77	5.8	12.0	5.2	6.2	-0.6
1950-59	6.1	12.7	5.3	6.6	-0.8
1960-69	4.2	13.4	6.6	9.2	2.4
1949-69	5.5	13.1	6.0	7.6	0.5
1970-78	6.6	9.4	3.3	2.8	-3.3
1972	4.7	10.7	4.5	6.0	-0.2
1973	5.8	10.3	3.8	4.5	-2.0
1974	7.7	7.9	1.5	0.2	-6.2
1975	8.5	8.3	2.8	-0.2	-5.7
1976	7.6	9.4	3.4	1.8	-4.2
1977	7.2	9.6	3.6	2.4	-3.6
1978	8.4	9.5	3.3	1.1	-5.1

Source: Cost of capital from Wenglowski; profit rates from table D4a.

narrowed and turned negative by as much as four percentage points by 1976, 1977 and 1978. This has registered two forces: 1) the acceleration in inflation, which gets translated into higher interest rates, and 2) a turn to more risk aversion as investors became increasingly fearful of the future of the economy and the policy decisions that the authorities might wish to adopt to curb inflation.

6 Rising Debt: The Emergence of Reduced Profitability

While the determinants of investment have been much studied, they remain imprecise in structural model formulation and forecasting power. Profitability clearly is important in the investment decision, as is growth of output or sales, capacity utilization rates, the rental price of capital, and q (the ratio of the market value of capital to its replacement cost).

As this study has indicated, the experience of the 1970s shows lowered profitability. Presumptively, this has affected the means by which corporations were able to finance investment. Multiple-factored in influence that the investment decision is subjected to, the ability to finance capital projects, especially from internal funds of corporations, would appear to have made some difference in the rate of capital formation in the 1970s. To the extent that profitability did diminish, the calculation of expected rates of return on proposed capital projects must have deterred, to some unknown volume, that expansion in capital formation that otherwise would have been expected in the 1970s, and which was not forthcoming.

The quantification of this deficiency is difficult and outside the scope of this study. Yet, the already cited evidence of slow-up in the growth of the stock of capital per se, as well as in relation to labor in the 1970s, and especially since 1973, indicates that elements of deterence to capital investment have been important.

In part, of course, the expansion in capital facilities in the early 1970s, combined with the sharp recession of 1974-75, appeared to generate a certain ampleness of production facilities; operating rates in manufacturing appeared very comfortable in those years. Nevertheless, as the economic expansion developed from the cyclical trough in March 1975, much of the excess capacity was rapidly used up in many manufacturing sectors. The several measures of operating rates are shown in table 6.1.

By the last part of 1978, only two percentage points represented the excess of production potential from the inflation-prone, pressure-filled

Table 6.1. Capacity Utilization in Manufacturing
(percent)

	Federal Reserve	Commerce Department	Wharton
1973	87.5	86	93.4
1974	84.2	83	90.9
1975	73.6	77	80.3
1976	80.2	81	86.6
1977	82.4	83	89.1
1978	84.2	84	92.5
1978 IV.	85.9	84	94.0

Sources: Board of Governors of the Federal Reserve System, Department of Commerce, and Wharton School of Finance.

year of 1973, according to Federal Reserve estimates. Indeed, the Wharton School measure of capacity utilization in late 1978 had surpassed the 1973 rate. The slower growth in capital stock was a direct precondition of rapid buildup in operating rates in manufacturing in 1976-78.

Taking the 1970s as a whole, a convincing argument can be made that these were generally years of high employment, strong aggregate demand, and inflationary pressures. If factors are to be sought for explaining reduced growth in capital stock, a presumption exists that it was not because strong aggregate demand was lacking, viewing these years as a composite. (Indeed, a belated consensus that the inflation was demand-pull in basic nature, though perhaps not of the classical variety, finally emerged in late 1978. Official economic policy appeared tardy in embracing fiscal and monetary restraint, higher interest rates, and "voluntary" wage and price guidelines).

SOURCES OF INTERNAL FUNDS

Funds which become available to corporations from internal sources may be variously defined as 1) "book" profits after taxes (typically reported before adjustment for replacement cost of inventories and depreciation), plus capital consumption allowances 2) as in 1) above, exclusive of dividends paid; 3) NIPA profits after taxes (as adjusted for replacement cost of inventories and depreciation, described in detail in Chapter 2), plus capital consumption allowances; 4) as in 3) above, with exclusion of dividends paid.

In determining what might be available to corporations from internally generated funds, at least the following three considerations would hold:

- Book or reported profits overstate economic profits when understatement of the replacement cost of inventories and depreciation develops during periods of inflation. Accordingly, the trend of profitability is better represented by figures which make allowances for true replacement costs. Hence, the official national accounts data (NIPA), which attempt to adjust profits for replacement cost, would appear to be more valid measures of funds available for investment. The "book" dollars are there – but in a true economic sense, they have been committed. (NIPA profits are sometimes designed "operating profits".)

–   A second consideration is whether profits after taxes (NIPA) but before payment of dividends, rather than retained earnings, might be considered as internal funds available for finance. The official Economic Report of the President (1978) includes such a concept. To a degree, dividends are a matter of company policy which may be changed to secure more funds from internal sources as needed. However, this would not apply to a large number of corporations which view payment of dividends as much a means of attracting capital as the payment of interest on debt instruments. The resistance to change in the absolute volume of dividends during recession years would support this view.

–   The inclusion of capital consumption allowances as part of internal sources of funds is less controversial – though not absent of it. Depreciation is a cost, albeit a noncash cost; and, of course, sums of money become available as depreciation is charged. They are to be used for whatever purposes companies may choose; indeed, they are potentially available to finance investment or other uses. Yet, the fact that payment for such costs does not occur at a particular point in time should not be considered as more than a temporary respite. Indeed, depreciation might be viewed as little different than any other deferred expense which contributes to current "cash flow," but is not really available when longer term costs are considered. From the standpoint of an ongoing enterprise, the cost of replacement of physical capital must be met sooner or later.

In the 1974 language of the Concepts and Standards Committee of the American Accounting Association:

Income from ordinary operations should represent an amount, in current dollars, which . . . is available for distribution outside the firm without contraction of its operating capacity; or, stated in another way, the amount which by retention is available for expansion of operating capacity . . . That is, in order to continue operations without contracting the level of operating capacity, exhausted services must be restored; the relevant cost of expired services is the current cost of restoration.

Viewed over the longer period, depreciation and the cash it generated cannot be allocated for purposes of higher wages or dividends. If it were given to stockholders, it would reduce the capital of the firm which, as an ongoing enterprise, would need to replace cash from these funds by other sources. At best, funds accruing from depreciation allowances, which become available as a source of finance, are so accumulated to replace existing plant or equipment. Depreciation allowances may do little to provide financing for the expansion of the net stock of capital.

Often enough, of course, mere replacement of physical capital introduces a production potential that is greater than had existed earlier, because the state of technology has advanced since the capital facility had been originally set in place. The cost of replacement, moreover, may have diminished, if new methods of capital goods production had been developed and registered in lower prices of capital goods.

These factors, however, need to be considered in the light of the typically understated replacement cost of depreciation due to inflation. Depreciation at original cost cannot cover the funds needed to replace physical assets affected by inflation since the mid-1960s. In any event, the availability of funds from depreciation allowances would appear to be much more important in satisfying replacement capital requirements, rather than expansion in the net stock.

RETAINED EARNINGS IN PERSPECTIVE

The adequacy of corporate earnings to finance working and fixed capital since the mid-1960s appears to have declined substantially by the standards of so-called economic profits after taxes and retained earnings. As previously indicated, book profits surely do not represent a guide to the adequacy of generation of internal funds, because of the use of historical rather than replacement cost in adjustments for inventory change and depreciation charges. If capital consumption allowances are considered as designed only for replacement of capital, then a concept which centers on retained earnings would appear justified for use as a measure of funds which become available for financing of increases in the net stock of capital.

In table 6.2, profits after taxes have been adjusted by NIPA allowances for replacement cost of inventory and depreciation. To a large degree, the adjustment to a NIPA basis of depreciation has minimized the arbitrariness frequently ascribed to depreciation schedules – a procedure described in Chapter 2. Even so, the present method of straight-line depreciation is relatively crude in determining economic depreciation, though an improvement over the older procedure. Profit measures, accordingly, have been much improved – surely in terms of consistency, if not accuracy. The surprising result in the table's figures is that for the 1970-78 period, the volume of profits after taxes is only 21 percent higher than in 1960-69, while GNP has more than doubled.

When attention is directed to retained earnings, as here adjusted, the sqeeze on internally generated and available funds for expansion of investment is even more striking, as shown in figure 6.1 Retained

Table 6.2. Nonfinancial Corporations: "Adjusted" Gross Saving
(billion dollars)

Averages	Profits After Tax (NIPA)	Dividends	"Adjusted" Retained Earnings	Capital Consumption Allowances, Adjusted	Gross Saving*
1948-78	26.6	16.8	9.8	42.8	53.9
1950-59	14.5	9.1	5.4	19.3	25.9
1960-69	31.2	16.1	15.1	34.3	49.4
1970-78	37.9	28.6	9.3	85.4	107.0
1976	48.4	33.5	14.9	106.7	121.6
1977	55.0	39.1	15.9	115.6	131.5
1978	56.5	45.0	11.5	126.5	138.0

*Detail may not add to total, due to rounding.
Source: U.S. Department of Commerce

earnings at $9 billion averaged annually during 1970-1978 were lower than in 1960-69, despite the huge expansion in GNP over that period.

The years 1976 and 1977 brought substantial improvement to the profit performance. Even so, retained earnings at $16 billion in 1977 were virtually equal only to the average of 1960-69, while 1978 registered lower.

"ADJUSTED" RETAINED EARNINGS
WITH DOUBLE-DECLINING DEPRECIATION

As noted earlier, depreciation charges are difficult to ascertain. The service life of any physical asset might be estimated differently; moreover, the curve in the stream of services over an asset's life might

Table 6.3. Nonfinancial Corporations:
"Adjusted" Retained Earnings
(bil. dol.)

Averages	With "Straight Line" Depreciation	With Double-Declining Balance Depreciation
1948-78	9.8	7.0
1950-59	5.4	4.1
1960-69	15.1	12.7
1970-78	9.3	4.0
1976	14.9	9.8
1977	15.9	10.5
1978	11.5	5.2

Source: U.S. Department of Commerce.

$ Billion

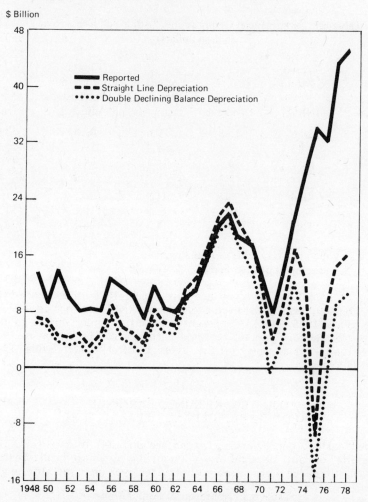

Fig. 6.1. Retained earnings, reported and adjusted for IVA and replacement cost of depreciation (nonfinancial corporations).

also be subject to conjecture. The estimates of "adjusted" retained earnings (and of capital consumption) in table 6.2 were based on the officially assumed 85 percent of IRS's Bulletin F service lives and straight-line depreciation. If a "double-declining balance" method of depreciation had been applied, the "adjusted" retained earnings would have registered even lower for the 1970s as shown in table 6.3.

The superiority of the double-declining balance method has been argued persuasively by Terborgh (1954) and others. Admittedly, it is more applicable to equipment (which accounts for four-fifths of depreciation) than to structures. Obviously, it follows that computations of so-called "cash flow" (or gross savings), which might use double-declining balance methods, would tend to be smaller in recent years than the official estimates.

THE "CASH FLOW" ESTIMATES

The add-back of capital consumption allowances (including the "capital consumption adjustment" to capture changes in the replacement cost of capital) to retained earnings in order to obtain "gross saving" does brighten a financial picture that might otherwise be considered quite dismal. It has been argued that charging depreciation is a fairly arbitrary procedure; and such charges should be considered part of profits. That view misapprehends the fundamental nature of depreciation as other than a cost, because it would need in some sense to be deducted from, not added to, profits for the reasons stated above.

Of course, a sum of money does become available from depreciation charges which might be considered a factor in financing fixed investment. But that sum might also be used to finance inventories, receivables, or even retirement of debt. Indeed, as an alternative, borrowed funds might be used for any of these, as well as for other purposes, but that would not change the nature of its status as a claim by creditors.

Nevertheless, internally generated funds in some sense might provide a psychological atmosphere that would affect the investment decision. Borrowed funds generally are a less favored financing means for investment than internal funds, despite tax advantages of the former. But that is not a compelling argument in the view of this study.

In table 6.4, a measure of profitability is presented in terms of NIPA profits after taxes as a percent of gross domestic product. This, as has been observed, shows a dramatic decline in the 1970s. Cash flow or gross saving, however, does not fall so dramatically because depreciation charges have increased enormously in recent years. In 1970-77, capital consumption charges were 80 percent of gross saving. By 1977 and 1978, they were about 90 percent of gross saving. Nevertheless,

Table 6.4. Nonfinancial Corporations:
NIPA Profits After Taxes as a
Percent of Gross Domestic Product

Averages	Profits After Taxes (NIPA)	Gross Saving	Ratio: Plant & Equipment Outlays to Gross Saving*
1948-78	6.8	12.0	1.0
1950-59	7.0	11.8	1.0
1960-1969	8.0	12.8	1.0
1970-78	4.5	11.1	1.2

*Nonfarm, nonfinancial corporate business.
Source: U.S. Department of Commerce and Federal Reserve.

these are committed funds, so to speak, to be viewed as replacement costs and not really available for the finance of expansion of net capital formation.

As table 6.4 shows, while after-tax profit as a share of product was halved in 1970-77, as compared with the 1960s, gross saving declined by about one-eighth.

Recognizing the frailties of this measure, a so-called "financing gap" might be considered – the relationship of plant and equipment expenditures to gross saving. As shown in table 6.4, the earlier postwar years gradually show that gross saving approximated expenditures on plant and equipment. The 1970s, however, represent a period when such outlays averaged 15 percent more than gross savings.

The perspective provided by the annual figures of figure 6.2 is more informative. In that figure capital expenditures have been defined as inclusive of investment in inventories, as well as in plant and equipment. In the 1960s and into the early 1970s, the financing gap was very large, reflecting the low levels of retained earnings and strong investment expenditures. In the mid-1970s, the gap diminished considerably, as investment outlays lagged. As the latter accelerated in 1976 and 1977, a financing gap again appeared. In 1977, that gap was one-fifth more than available internal funds. In 1978, the gap promises to be one-third more than those funds. For the 1970-78 period, as a whole, capital expenditures averaged 31 percent more than internal funds generated.

DEBT-FINANCING AS A SOURCE OF FUNDS

Since the 1960s, the growth of debt incurred by nonfinancial corporations has proceeded at a phenomenal rate. In part, this was associated with the pressures exerted by the slow-up in profitability which, as has been shown, reduced the adequacy of corporate earnings to finance working and fixed capital requirements. As internal funds became less available, external sources were sought.

By some standards, debt financing merely represents an alternative source of funds available in capital markets at a price – the interest rate. Indeed, in view of the so-called "leverage" it provides to equity-owners, and its preferential tax treatment, debt might be, and has been considered, a desirable form of finance.

Yet, it is not merely that. From a public policy view, growth of corporate debt may represent an ominous development because it raises break-even points in profitability, makes business more vulnerable to cyclical downturns, and tends to shorten the magnitude and direction of cyclical expansions. From the standpoint of individual enterprise, it makes more fragile the latter's ability to weather unexpected vicissitudes that are frequently encountered in business. It introduces a fixed cost element that is as burdensome as other fixed costs during periods of economic stagnation and contraction. (The inflation, of course, lightens the burden of this debt, as it is repaid by cheaper dollars. As indicated previously, however, the net advantage of inflation to

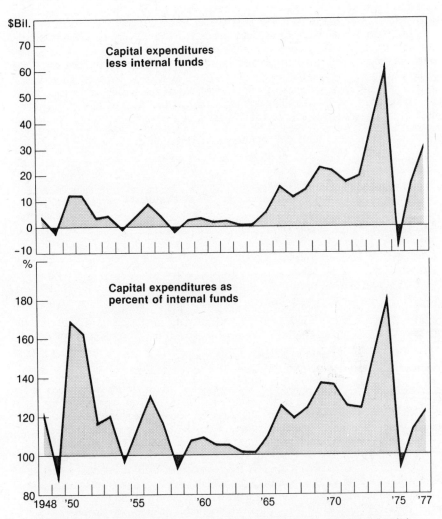

Note: Internal funds are sum of retained earnings, adjusted for inventory valuation and capital consumption allowances, including capital consumption adjustment (NIPA). Capital expenditures are sum of outlays for business fixed investment, inventories and minor items.

Fig. 6.2. Financing gap: nonfinancial corporations.

corporations may not be decisive if pension reserve losses and income on outstanding debt outweigh gains from inflation on debt.)

Total outstanding credit market liabilities (bonds, mortgages, bank loans, and other credit instruments) in relation to gross product originating rose to a high of 69 percent during 1970-78. This compared with 58 percent in 1960-69 and as little as 50 percent in the 1950s.

An alternative measure of debt burden is the ability to service debt out of current production or profit, on the presumption that as long as interest payments are in some favorable relation with present or potential income no difficulty would arise from debt burden. However, as table 6.5 shows, interest paid in relation to the value of output has advanced sharply. In 1970-78, this ratio was triple that of the 1950s and half as much again as that of the 1960s.

Table 6.5. Nonfinancial Corporations:
Measures of Debt Burden

Averages	Outstanding Debt as Percent of Gross Product Originating	Net Interest Paid as Percent of:	
		Gross Product Originating	Profits Before Tax (NIPA)
1948-78	57.9	1.7	20.2
1950-59	49.7	.8	5.2
1960-69	58.3	1.7	11.5
1970-78	69.0	2.6	33.3
1976	68.1	3.1	30.3
1977	68.0	3.1	29.6
1978	67.2	3.0	29.7

Note: Detail may not add to totals due to rounding.
Source: U.S. Department of Commerce and Federal Reserve.

These ratios might appear low, even at their increased value of recent years. Presumably, the interest costs are at the expense of profits. One such measure of the drag on profits exerted by interest costs also is shown in the table. For 1970-78, interest payments represented one-third of profits before tax (on the NIPA basis). This is three times the share of the 1960s and six times that of the 1950s.

Of course, no danger point in the volume of debt to product can be established reliably. Presumably, the underlying condition for safety is a steady rise in corporate earnings, as well as continuation of expansionary monetary and fiscal policies, which create no problem for incurrence of new or rollover of old debt.

The monetary authorities, of course, may continue to supply financial resources to the credit markets, which would defer the problem generated by expansion of debt. Indeed, it has been the concern by the authorities that curbing of credit expansion might result in slowup in economic growth that has prolonged the cyclical expansion that started in early 1975. Growth in the monetary aggregates that has far exceeded that of real gross national product has made possible expanded credit use – indeed, the latter is merely an image of the former.

DEBT-EQUITY RELATIONSHIPS

The expansion of debt, in part, has been motivated by the lack of viable alternatives: the relatively lesser volume available from internal funds and, most importantly, the poor performance in the stock market. With stocks of many companies selling below book values, which is expressed generally by the decline in the q measure discussed earlier, the issuance of new stocks has been sharply discouraged. Moreover, on the demand side, a shift in portfolios by institutional investors out of equities and into debt has developed, as assurance of income has become more prized. Since 1974, private pension funds have decreased their investment in stocks from about 70 percent of their funds to 50 percent in 1977.

The Changing Debt-Equity Relationship

Another view of debt is its changed relationship to equity as a source of funds in the structure of the balance sheet. The mounting burden of debt is clearly evidenced in the ratios shown in the third column of table 6.6. By 1978, the total of credit market instruments — mainly bonds, mortgages, bank loans, and commercial paper — had reached 834 billion. This was three and one half times that in the 1960s. In contrast, net worth at book or historical value had advanced two and one half times.

Table 6.6. Nonfinancial Corporations:
Debt-Equity Ratio

Averages	Credit Market Liabilities	Stockholder's Equity	Percent Ratio*
	(bil. dol.)		$(1) \div (2)$
	(1)	(2)	(3)
1950-59	104.5	203.6	51.1
1960-69	227.6	356.2	63.0
1970-77	582.3	664.2	86.9
1976	673.6	775.2	86.9
1977	749.7	828.9	90.4
1978	834.2	902.2	92.5

*Figures may not add to totals due to rounding.
Source: Federal Reserve "Flow of Funds"

As a result, a new debt-equity relationship has emerged. Outstanding debt was equal to 92 percent of equity in 1978, which was not only higher than the 87 percent level of the earlier 1970s but was substantially above the 63 percent averaged in the 1960s.

As a measure of financial health, it is clear that the greater the debt-equity ratio, the more vulnerable is corporate enterprise. By and large, this would not appear to represent a significant hazard for the largest corporations; indeed, it was not so during the critical recession period of 1974-75. Those companies appeared to be in even stronger position in 1978; there were many "cash-rich" companies in that year. Yet, the problem of increased rigidities resulting from the added element of an additional fixed cost involving the service of the debt is not easily minimized for most corporations. For many, it surely would make a large difference with respect to survival should recession or even slow growth in the economy emerge. The lag in investment in plant and equipment and the cautious building of inventories during the expansion beginning in 1975 is a reflection of careful management of available financial resources.

In this connection, the liquidity ratios of companies would make the difference on survival chances. Corporations in recent years are less liquid financially than formerly and, therefore, would be vulnerable to cyclical downturns. Of course, long-term developments in better management of liquid assets has been reflected in a steady downtrend in most working capital ratios. This may be observed in the ratio of liquid assets of short-term liabilities. This trend presumably has extended into the 1970s. It is nevertheless of some concern that the 1970-78 ratio had descended to 28.5, which compares with 38.7 in the 1960-69 period and values above 50 in the 1950s. (In 1978, the ratio has edged downward again).

The continued advance in debt represents a disturbing, if not worrisome, element in the financial position of corporations. The increased reliance on debt financing raises the potential for difficulty in obtaining external funds, should the monetary authorities move to a policy of credit stringency as part of an antiinflation program. Credit "crunches" are much less avoidable under these circumstances.

7 General Conclusions and Policy Implications

The findings of this study established that profitability of nonfinancial corporations — interpreted in great definitional variety — has declined substantially during the 1970s.

Whether defined on a before- or after-tax profit basis, or with respect to alternative concepts of total or physical assets or net worth, profitability has moved lower, especially since the mid-1960s. Energy and other special factors in the 1970s have contributed only transiently to reduced profitability because market pressures of adjustment to other cost pressures also have been inadequate.

First and most obviously, the ravages of inflation on book or reported profits have been severe in recent years and do not correctly state profitability as such, nor return on investment. When corrections for replacement costs of inventory and depreciation are made, corporate profitability in the 1970s was low.

Moreover, cyclical adjustments that purport to raise profitability that might be expected at full employment do not raise rates of return significantly: they remain below that of the 1960s and the 1950s. Indeed, as estimates of potential GNP are revised down, as they were in 1977, 1978, and 1979, the magnitude of the cyclical adjustments becomes smaller and adjusted rates tend to be closer to the actual rates. Since that is so, the deterioration shown in the actual profitability rates, which is conceded generally, is confirmed as bearing the essential message of a shift to a lowered rate of return on investment since the mid-1960s. This is a development which would appear ominous in its implications for the incentive to invest. Consequently, the attainment of a change in the allocation of resources towards more investment appears less felicitous than it might otherwise be.

Granted that strong aggregate demand is a necessary condition that favors investment, the incentive to invest is surely affected by sufficiency of funds to finance it, and by encouragement of the commitment of those funds in terms of a return on investment.

Accordingly, the finding of this study that profitability has declined must stand the test of whether it is sufficiently long-standing to cause concern and to require remedial policy action; or whether some automatic correction will come during a normal evolution towards higher rates of business activity. Under these latter circumstances, little or no change in economic policy would be required. However, the high levels of economic activity in 1977 and 1978 did not restore profitability to former levels; indeed, they remained far below those predicted by studies that had used cyclical adjustments. Since high economic activity and employment in 1977 and 1978 did not restore corporate earnings to rates favorable for sustained investment, further stimulative general economic policies would appear inappropriate for this purpose.

Some fundamental structural shift since the mid-1960s lies underneath the reduced profitability rates. Basic cost-price relationships appear to have experienced considerable change, being expressed in a smaller share of profits in relation to national income and product and a larger share of labor compensation. In recent years, the labor compensation share – defined not only as wages and salaries but as total labor costs, including fringe benefits and social security taxes – appears to have increased more than the share of most other major factor receipts. On top of that have been the relatively higher real costs of energy and of environmental protection, which have not been translated fully in price adjustments. Accordingly, profit margins have turned lower, surely in comparison with the mid-1960s.

A clear explanation of this is observed in the 1973-78 experience of contribution to inflation by factor shares. Unit labor costs at nonfinancial corporations contributed 5.1 percent annually to the price increase of 7.4 percent, while unit profits before taxes contributed only 0.6 percent, as table D2b shows. In 1978, the comparable advances were a unit labor cost increase of 5.4 percent, a price advance of 6.8 percent, and a unit profit rise of 0.4 percent. Over the entire span since 1967, the squeeze was reflected in a price advance of 92 percent and a unit profit rise of only 25 percent.

The inadequacy of profit rates on a long-term basis emerged in the late 1960s, rather than in the 1970s, as other studies have alleged. Precisely at that time, productivity turned lower and reduced the buffer that wage demands exert on prices. Profit margins turned narrower, making returns on investment less attractive. Growth in capital formation diminished, and so did productivity. Thus, lower profitability was associated with a reduction in productivity, which, in turn, reflected lowered rates of capital formation.

As noted earlier, the emergence of reduced profit margins and lowered rates of return has reflected an inadequate market adjustment to increases in relative real costs of labor and other types of costs, including those associated with energy and the environment. In a sense, price adjustments to account for these higher costs have not developed because of real or imagined fears of government intervention, price controls, import competition, and other factors.

A dilemma is thereby posed: whether the adjustment should be reflected in price increases which encourage the inflation that has been proceeding at an unacceptable rate, or whether efforts that would accomplish this adjustment should proceed through measures to restrain the inflation by demand management. The alternative of direct controls of wages and prices would be a third and "worst-case" solution.

Another method of resolving the dilemma is by providing some inspiration for increased investment which would provide the increased productivity that might dampen increases in unit labor costs. Rising input costs of labor might normally trigger a move towards more capital-intensive production. In fact, that has not occurred. This is evident by the slow-up in growth in the capital stock in recent years, as shown in table 7.1.

Table 7.1. Nonfarm Business Sector
Percent, Average Annual Growth

	Capital Stock	Hours	Labor Productivity	Change in Net Capital-Labor Ratio
1948-55	3.0	1.0	2.8	1.9
1955-65	3.2	1.0	2.6	2.2
1965-73	4.5	1.8	2.0	2.6
1973-77	2.4	1.5	0.8	0.9

Table 7.1 also indicates the decline in productivity growth in recent years, which may be presumed to have been the link with slowed growth of capital stock.

Obviously, tax policies which would promote after-tax profitability would represent a step in this direction, as discussed subsequently. But even these measures would not suffice unless two uncertainties are resolved: 1) those relating to assurances concerning the containment of inflation which would operate to lower the risk premium now perceived and, 2) those relating to the energy and environmental factors which have operated to delay decisions on plant design and construction.

These changes in public policies — through tax and other measures — appear required to provide greater incentive to invest. In any event, reliance on orthodox macropolicy to achieve higher utilization rates in the economy as a means of restoring profitability, may prove unrealistic and self-defeating. A shift to lower productivity has occurred with negative implications for profitability, it may persist for awhile and could be helped by increased investment.

The acceleration of inflation has complicated the problem of incentive to invest — through the channels of increasing the cost of capital, raising effective tax rates, and marking up the risk factor. Indeed, a case for steady policies directed towards deceleration of inflation would do much to blunt the force of these factors. The reduction in inflation surely would represent an added incentive towards changing the mix of consumption and saving. Under conditions of prudent demand management, increased saving would provide a basis for meeting the twin goals of increased standards of living and continued reduction in inflation.

The Road to More Capital Formation – and Less Inflation

Now that the damage is done, the inflation outlook over the next several years appears bleak and, perhaps, irrevocable without Draconian measures. The declining trends in productivity, the potentially strong wage pressures and the reduced rates of return on corporate capital contribute to an inflation-prone outlook for the economy. However, long-term prospects could be brighter under other conditions that might be sought. Public policies directed towards harnessing the energies and incentives of the private sector in support of higher rates of capital formation would appear to provide the long-term solution to the inflation-productivity nexus. Short-term measures by the Congress and several recent Administrators to avert recessions have brought neither disinflation nor stability.

To provide the felicitous atmosphere for increased rates of capital formation and set the Nation on the road to disinflation, increased saving by the Nation would be required.

The potential sources of increased saving are three-fold:

- Moderating the growth of Government expenditures. The share of Government purchases of goods and services plus transfer payments to individuals has increased to nearly one-third in the 1970s, as compared with one-fourth in the 1960s. Reducing this share would contribute to smaller deficits or generate surpluses; drains on private saving would be reduced and necessarily be freed to provide the sources of financing in private sector investment. Of course, not all Government spending is without contribution to general productivity, though reasonable persons would agree that markets in the private sector exert a discipline not usually present in public enterprises.

- Increasing corporate saving. While the share of private domestic investment to GNP has not declined dramatically, growth in the stock of capital and in capital-labor ratios have diminished and reduced productivity, as noted previously. Rewards to corporate enterprise need to be restored, perhaps to the level of the 1960s. Changes in tax rates would represent one means of attaining this objective – changes in depreciation allowances is another – though this study has indicated that pretax returns have turned low by historical standards. (Investment tax credits are said to be preferable and more efficient than tax rate reduction in stimulating investment, though the latter surely would be conducive even indirectly in the process of enlarging the economy's saving).

- Rewards for saving by individuals are intimately related to those of corporate enterprise and should respond to increases in the latter's rate of return. Rising income may be accompanied by rising saving in conventional economic analysis, though that doctrine does not exclude calculations of benefits from deferred consumption.

A host of other measures need to be considered in productivity growth. However, this study would conclude that reduced rates of return to corporate enterprise have significantly contributed to lowered rates of capital formation and productivity growth.

In the meantime, the message of inadequate rates of return to corporations has been blurred. Corporate profits continue to be reported on the basis of book or historical costs, which falsely bloats them and makes it appear that corporations are reluctant dragons, or perverse in some fashion, in undertaking investment. Accordingly, the genuine need for more corporate saving, as is frequently expressed by corporate officers, needs to be supported by changes in methods of reporting profits towards placing their accounting statements on a more realistic basis.

That is only, and simply, a matter of valid methods of accounting during a period of inflation. Having established that properly accounted profits are much less than reported, the second step is the acceptance of the conclusion of this study that profitability has declined on a secular basis. Finally, economic and social policy needs to provide a remedy for this condition, if capital formation is to increase in growth.

Statistical Appendix

Table A. Glossary of Variables

NIPINT	Profits before tax (NIPA) plus interest as percent of depreciable capital.
PATINT	Profits after tax (NIPA) plus interest as percent of depreciable capital.
ZBAB	Profits before tax (NIPA) as percent of depreciable capital.
PATJSL	Profits after tax (NIPA) as percent of depreciable capital.
ZBDINT	Profits before tax plus interest (double declining balance depreciation) as percent of depreciable capital.
PADIMT	Profits after tax plus interest (double declining balance depreciation) as percent of depreciable capital.
ZBDDB	Profits before tax (double declining balance depreciation) as percent of depreciable capital.
PATJD	Profits after tax (double declining balance depreciation) as percent of depreciable capital.
Q GAP	Perloff-Wachter gap below potential GNP.
STL GAP	St. Louis Federal Reserve GNP gap.
CEA GAP	Council of Economic Advisors GNP gap.
TR GAP	Trend GNP gap, Boshan and Ebanks
UCAP FR	Capacity Utilization rate in manufacturing, Federal Reserve.
UCAP WN	Capacity Utilization rate in manufacturing, Wharton EFU
D60	Dummy variable, with 1962-68 values at 1, other years at 0.
D65, TD65	Dummy variables with intercept and slope change at 1965.
D70, TD70	Dummy variables with intercept and slope change at 1970.

Table B1. Trends in the Rate of Return to Nonfinancial Corporate Capital, 1950-77: Profits Before Taxes (NIPA) Plus Interest

| | | | INDEPENDENT VARIABLES | | | | REGRESSION STATISTICS | | | |
| | Constant | | GAP | | UCAP | | | | | |
Equation	Coefficient	Time	CEA	STL	FR	W	RHO	$\bar{R}^2$	DW	SEE
A.	13.440 (6.165)	-0.118 (-1.033)					0.702 (5.115)	0.612	1.786	1.383
B.	-28.241 (-2.964)	-0.034 (-0.377)	0.411 (4.442)				0.706 (5.182)	0.778	1.322	1.046
C.	-44.835 (-5.018)	-0.097 (-2.159)		0.590 (6.583)			0.522 (3.178)	0.846	1.529	0.871
D.	-4.255 (-0.947)	-0.096 (-1.222)			0.208 (4.189)		0.664 (4.611)	0.766	1.664	1.075
E.	-0.817 (-0.187)	-0.149 (-1.372)				0.167 (3.704)	0.742 (5.756)	0.742	1.644	1.128

Note: Figures in parenthesis are "t"-statistics. See table A for designation of variables.

Table B2. Trends in the Rate of Return to Nonfinancial
Corporate Capital, 1950-77: Profits Before Taxes (NIPA)

Equation	Constant Coefficient	Time	INDEPENDENT VARIABLES GAP CEA	STL	UCAP FR	W	RHO	$\bar{R}^2$	DW	SEE
A.	13.504 (5.914)	-0.213 (-1.771)					0.702 (5.126)	0.716	1.781	1.445
B.	-28.722 (-2.812)	-0.123 (-1.186)	0.416 (4.206)				0.728 (5.511)	0.830	1.362	1.120
C.	-45.146 (-4.623)	-0.188 (-3.561)		0.593 (6.058)			0.557 (3.483)	0.878	1.585	0.948
D.	-4.225 (-0.875)	-0.189 (-2.183)			0.208 (3.912)		0.671 (4.704)	0.819	1.698	1.154
E.	-0.673 (0.144)	-0.244 (-2.109)				0.166 (3.444)	0.744 (5.788)	0.802	1.675	1.208

REGRESSION STATISTICS

Note: Figures in parenthesis are "t"-statistics. See table A for designation of variables.

89

Table B3. Trends in the Rate of Return to Nonfinancial Corporate Capital, 1950-77: Profits After Taxes (NIPA) Plus Interest

| Equation | Constant Coefficient | INDEPENDENT VARIABLES | | | | | REGRESSION STATISTICS | | | |
		Time	GAP CEA	STL	UCAP FR	W	RHO	$\bar{R}^2$	DW	SEE
A.	6.274 (2.826)	0.007 (0.060)					0.786 (6.616)	0.601	1.606	0.952
B.	-11.447 (-1.416)	0.046 (0.493)	0.174 (2.250)				0.765 (6.177)	0.656	1.523	0.884
C.	-20.060 (-2.344)	0.024 (0.350)		0.265 (3.114)			0.702 (5.125)	0.698	1.727	0.828
D.	-0.291 (-0.074)	-0.019 (0.199)			0.076 (1.885)		0.761 (6.086)	0.637	1.710	0.908
E.	1.251 (0.335)	-0.007 (-0.064)				0.060 (1.646)	0.786 (6.615)	0.627	1.696	0.921

Note: Figures in parenthesis are "t" statistics. See table A for designation of variables.

Table B4. Trends in the Rate of Return to Nonfinancial Corporate Capital, 1950-77: Profits After Taxes (NIPA)

| | | | INDEPENDENT VARIABLES | | | | REGRESSION STATISTICS | | | |
| | | | GAP | | UCAP | | | | | |
Equation	Constant Coefficient	Time	CEA	STL	FR	W	RHO	$\bar{R}$-2	DW	SEE
A.	6.345 (2.749)	-0.087 (-0.759)					0.783 (6.542)	0.646	1.618	1.008
B.	-12.378 (-1.445)	-0.045 (-0.431)	0.184 (2.250)				0.775 (6.363)	0.695	1.525	0.935
C.	-21.824 (-2.429)	-0.068 (-0.927)		0.283 (3.170)			0.712 (5.265)	0.736	1.741	0.870
D.	-0.774 (-0.186)	-0.074 (-0.748)			0.083 (1.936)		0.761 (6.100)	0.680	1.717	0.957
E.	0.919 (0.233)	-0.102 (-0.899)				0.064 (1.687)	0.787 (6.634)	0.670	1.699	0.972

Note: Figures in parenthesis are "t" statistics. See table A for designation of variables.

Table B5. Trends in the Rate of Return to Nonfinancial Corporate Capital, 1950-77: Profits Before Taxes (Double Declining Balance Depreciation) Plus Interest

Equation	Constant Coefficient	Time	GAP		UCAP		REGRESSION STATISTICS			
			CEA	STL	FR	W	RHO	$\bar{R}^2$	DW	SEE
A.	13.005 (6.132)	-0.118 (-1.053)					0.691 (4.963)	0.604	1.786	1.403
B.	-28.716 (-2.934)	-0.031 (-0.335)	0.411 (4.326)				0.710 (5.232)	0.768	1.356	1.074
C.	-44.964 (-4.865)	-0.098 (-2.084)		0.587 (6.330)			0.526 (3.211)	0.837	1.586	0.901
D.	-4.686 (-1.016)	-0.097 (-1.239)			0.208 (4.063)		0.651 (4.458)	0.755	1.698	1.104
E.	-1.095 (-0.246)	-0.147 (-1.384)				0.165 (3.535)	0.733 (5.592)	0.728	1.666	1.163

Note: Figures in parenthesis are "t" statistics. See table A for designation of variables.

Table B6. Trends in the Rate of Return to Nonfinancial Corporate Capital, 1950-77: Profits Before Taxes (Double Declining Balance Depreciation)

| | | | INDEPENDENT VARIABLES | | | | REGRESSION STATISTICS | | | |
| | | | GAP | | UCAP | | | | | |
Equation	Constant Coefficient	Time	CEA	STL	FR	W	RHO	$\bar{R}^2$	DW	SEE
A.	13.040 (5.894)	-0.211 (-1.807)					0.693 (4.990)	0.713	1.781	1.454
B.	-29.199 (-2.824)	-0.119 (-1.124)	0.415 (4.153)				0.732 (5.580)	0.826	1.366	1.133
C.	-45.464 (-4.627)	-0.188 (-3.435)		0.591 (6.006)			0.569 (3.591)	0.877	1.590	0.952
D.	-4.842 (-0.998)	-0.188 (-2.203)			0.210 (3.916)		0.664 (4.613)	0.818	1.700	1.160
E.	-1.164 (-0.247)	-0.240 (-2.071)				0.166 (3.404)	0.740 (5.720)	0.798	1.670	1.221

Note: Figures in parenthesis are "t" statistics. See table A for designation of variables.

93

Table B7. Trends in the Rate of Return to Nonfinancial Corporate Capital, 1950-77: Profits After Taxes (Double Declining Balance Depreciation) Plus Interest

Equation	Constant Coefficient	Time	GAP CEA	GAP STL	UCAP FR	UCAP W	RHO	$\bar{R}^2$	DW	SEE
A.	5.744 (2.737)	0.013 (0.121)					0.773 (6.334)	0.583	1.633	0.965
B.	-12.378 (-1.514)	0.523 (0.555)	0.178 (2.275)				0.762 (6.116)	0.643	1.531	0.894
C.	-21.469 (-2.493)	0.028 (0.423)		0.274 (3.198)			0.691 (4.973)	0.690	1.740	0.833
D.	-1.230 (-0.313)	0.024 (0.269)			0.081 (1.985)		0.748 (5.855)	0.627	1.730	0.914
E.	0.471 (0.126)	-0.001 (-0.011)				0.062 (1.703)	0.778 (6.436)	0.613	1.709	0.931

INDEPENDENT VARIABLES / REGRESSION STATISTICS

Note: Figures in parenthesis are "t" statistics. See table A for designation of variables.

Table B8. Trends in the Rate of Return to Nonfinancial Corporate Capital,
1950-77: Profits After Taxes (Double Declining Balance Depreciation)

Equation	Constant Coefficient	INDEPENDENT VARIABLES					REGRESSION STATISTICS			
		Time	GAP		UCAP		RHO	$\bar{R}^2$	DW	SEE
			CEA	STL	FR	W				
A.	5.765 (2.625)	-0.079 (-0.718)					0.770 (6.269)	0.631	1.614	1.026
B.	-12.638 (-1.439)	-0.039 (-0.374)	0.181 (2.154)				0.767 (6.215)	0.678	1.525	0.959
C.	-22.330 (-2.419)	-0.063 (-0.868)		0.283 (3.080)			0.699 (5.080)	0.721	1.737	0.893
D.	-1.239 (-0.294)	-0.068 (-0.704)			0.082 (1.855)		0.748 (5.848)	0.663	1.710	0.980
E.	0.568 (0.142)	-0.093 (-0.843)				0.061 (1.564)	0.775 (6.380)	0.651	1.684	0.998

Note: Figures in parenthesis are "t" statistics. See table A for designation of variables.

Table B9. Trends in the Rate of Return to Nonfinancial
Corporate Capital, 1955–77: With Perloff-Wachter GNP Gaps

| Equation | INDEPENDENT VARIABLES | | | | REGRESSION STATISTICS | | | |
	Constant Coefficient	Time	QGAP	RHO	$\bar{R}^2$	DW	SEE
NIPINT	-31.675 (-3.220)	-0.128 (-0.988)	0.450 (4.645)	0.751 (5.333)	0.819	1.238	0.963
PATINT	-17.855 (-2.140)	-0.045 (-0.382)	0.253 (3.094)	0.766 (5.588)	0.740	1.495	0.816
ZBAD	-32.358 (-3.003)	-0.223 (-1.561)	0.453 (4.273)	0.753 (5.363)	0.845	1.309	1.055
PATJSL	-19.637 (-2.194)	-0.141 (-1.166)	0.267 (3.038)	0.758 (5.459)	0.776	1.515	0.876
ZBDINT	-32.133 (-3.123)	-0.115 (-0.852)	0.448 (4.421)	0.750 (5.315)	0.802	1.248	1.007
PADINT	-18.818 (-2.247)	-0.033 (-0.274)	0.257 (3.128)	0.772 (5.697)	0.733	1.412	0.819
ZBDDB	-33.048 (-2.999)	-0.209 (-1.401)	0.453 (4.182)	0.757 (5.437)	0.837	1.286	1.079
PATJD	-19.490 (-2.102)	-0.125 (-0.992)	0.259 (2.842)	0.760 (5.482)	0.758	1.452	0.907

Note: Figures in parenthesis are "t" statistics. See table A for designation of variables.

Table C1. Trends in the Rate of Return to Nonfinancial Corporate
Capital, 1950-77: Profits Before Taxes (NIPA) Plus Interest

Equation	Constant Coefficient	Time	GAP CEA	GAP STL	FR UCAP	DUMMY D65	DUMMY TD65	DUMMY D70	DUMMY TD70	RHO	$\bar{R}^2$	DW	SEE
A.	-29.830 (-3.167)	0.282 (1.842)	0.399 (4.386)			9.331 (2.622)	-0.604 (-2.734)			0.590 (3.797)	0.814	1.536	0.959
B.	-23.885 (-2.571)	0.075 (0.864)	0.360 (3.848)					-1.020 (-0.177)	-0.069 (-0.866)	0.518 (3.148)	0.791	1.540	1.014
C.	-44.798 (-5.060)	0.094 (1.120)		0.574 (6.448)		5.501 (2.438)	-0.366 (-2.841)			0.389 (2.197)	0.875	1.850	0.784
D.	-40.596 (-4.404)	-0.002 (-0.030)		0.539 (5.703)				1.802 (0.417)	-0.152 (-0.807)	0.405 (2.304)	0.855	1.677	0.846
E.	-6.492 (-1.475)	0.148 (1.182)			0.210 (4.287)	9.044 (2.955)	-0.546 (-2.937)			0.498 (2.982)	0.809	1.904	0.970
F.	-4.819 (-1.109)	0.055 (0.707)			0.200 (3.910)			2.910 (0.536)	-0.244 (-1.026)	0.460 (2.695)	0.792	1.830	1.013

INDEPENDENT VARIABLES

REGRESSION STATISTICS

Note: Figures in parenthesis are "t" statistics: See table A for designation of variables.

Table C2. Trends in the Rate of Return to Nonfinancial Corporate
Capital, 1950–77: Profits After Taxes (NIPA) Plus Interest

Equation	Constant Coefficient	Time	GAP CEA	GAP STL	FR UCAP	DUMMY D65	DUMMY TD65	DUMMY D70	DUMMY TD70	RHO	R̄²	DW	SEE
A.	-14.536 (-1.925)	0.334 (3.479)	0.180 (2.456)			9.178 (3.993)	-0.578 (-4.232)			0.468 (2.748)	0.750	1.627	0.752
B.	-9.521 (-1.232)	0.203 (2.960)	0.141 (1.811)					3.468 (0.738)	-0.264 (-1.260)	0.488 (2.909)	0.683	1.556	0.849
C.	-28.522 (-3.833)	0.248 (4.538)		0.332 (4.445)		6.780 (4.156)	-0.439 (-5.093)			0.193 (1.023)	0.809	1.914	0.659
D.	-21.530 (-2.586)	0.167 (3.256)		0.267 (3.131)				4.229 (1.119)	+0.279 (-1.706)	0.353 (1.960)	0.737	1.684	0.773
E.	-4.342 (-1.236)	0.269 (3.361)			0.099 2.480	9.231 (4.535)	-0.554 (-4.671)			(0.373) (2.087)	0.744	1.880	0.762
F.	-2.479 (-0.682)	0.196 (3.242)			0.084 (1.944)			4.854 (1.110)	-0.329 (-1.730)	0.417 (2.386)	0.684	1.734	0.848

INDEPENDENT VARIABLES / REGRESSION STATISTICS

Note: Figures in parenthesis are "t" statistics. See table A for designation of variables.

Table C3. Trends in the Rate of Return to Nonfinancial Corporate Capital, 1950-77: Profits Before Taxes (Double Declining Balance Depreciation) Plus Interest

Equation	Constant Coefficient	Time	GAP CEÂ	STL	FR UCAP	D65	DUMMY TD65	D70	TD70	RHO	$\bar{R}^2$	DW	SEE
A.	-30.599 (-3.101)	0.289 (1.723)	0.402 (4.216)			8.950 (2.312)	-0.590 (-2.440)			0.609 (3.988)	0.796	1.541	1.007
B.	-24.085 (-2.507)	0.063 (0.672)	0.359 (3.707)					-0.001 (-0.413)	(-0.002)	0.537 (3.304)	0.780	1.533	1.046
C.	-45.877 (-4.881)	0.097 (1.067)		0.580 (6.140)		4.960 (2.035)	-0.347 (-2.477)			0.402 (2.283)	0.860	1.846	0.834
D.	-40.419 (-4.174)	-0.012 (-0.178)		0.533 (5.375)				0.313 (0.068)	-0.087 (-0.432)	0.421 (2.414)	0.842	1.678	0.886
E.	-6.966 (-1.504)	0.150 (1.113)			0.210 (4.088)	8.521 (2.608)	-0.526 (-2.643)			0.506 (3.048)	0.790	1.892	1.021
F.	-4.844 (-1.074)	0.044 (0.540)			0.197 (3.701)			1.301 (0.230)	-0.174 (-0.698)	0.466 (2.738)	0.778	1.818	1.051

Note: Figures in parenthesis are "t" statistics. See table A for designation of variables.

Table C4. Trends in the Rate of Return to Nonfinancial Corporate Capital, 1950-77: Profits After Taxes (Double Declining Balance Depreciation) Plus Interest

| Equation | Constant Coefficient | INDEPENDENT VARIABLES | | | | | | | | REGRESSION STATISTICS | | | |
		Time	GAP CEA	GAP STL	FR UCAP	DUMMY D65	TD65	D70	TD70	RHO	$\bar{R}^2$	DW	SEE
A.	-15.162 (-1.937)	0.348 (3.319)	0.181 (2.376)			8.814 (3.530)	-0.570 (-3.800)			0.497 (2.978)	0.725	1.609	0.785
B.	-9.592 (-1.199)	0.191 (2.546)	0.138 (1.714)					2.301 (0.462)	-0.208 (-0.929)	0.520 (3.163)	0.659	1.551	0.873
C.	-29.442 (-3.789)	0.264 (4.428)		0.336 (4.303)		6.292 (3.609)	-0.430 (-4.599)			0.233 (1.245)	0.789	1.870	0.687
D.	-21.020 (-2.413)	0.158 (2.763)		0.258 (2.871)				3.169 (0.777)	-0.229 (-1.289)	0.405 (2.302)	0.714	1.661	0.800
E.	-5.125 (-1.417)	0.285 (3.301)			0.101 (2.478)	8.755 (4.028)	-0.545 (-4.258)			0.400 (2.268)	0.723	1.852	0.787
F.	-2.706 (-0.726)	0.186 (2.879)			0.082 (1.862)			3.621 (0.791)	-0.272 (-1.357)	0.441 (2.554)	0.662	1.714	0.869

Note: Figures in parenthesis are "t" statistics. See table A for designation of variables.

Table C5. Trends in the Rate of Return to Nonfinancial Corporate Capital, 1950-77: Profits Before Taxes (NIPA) Plus Interest, Single Dummy

Equation	Constant Coefficient	Time	INDEPENDENT VARIABLES						REGRESSION STATISTICS			
			GAP			UCAP						
			CEA	STL	TR	FR	NM	D60	RHO	$\bar{R}^2$	DW	SEE
A.	-18.788 (-2.445)	-0.089 (-2.667)	0.319 (4.175)					2.499 (4.763)	0.281 (1.519)	0.835	1.808	0.903
B.	-35.596 (-4.263)	-0.114 (-4.730)		0.495 (5.858)				1.689 (3.538)	0.200 (1.063)	0.883	1.927	0.761
C.	-21.872 (-2.021)	-0.123 (-3.239)			0.346 (3.245)			3.057 (5.246)	0.351 (1.946)	0.800	1.795	0.994
D.	-3.503 (-0.905)	-0.123 (-4.273)				0.199 (4.361)		2.428 (4.803)	0.228 (1.216)	0.840	1.998	0.887
E.	0.482 (0.148)	-0.171 (-5.862)					0.149 (3.977)	2.950 (6.072)	0.201 (1.068)	0.827	1.944	0.924

Note: Figures in parenthesis are "t" statistics. See table A for designation of variables.

101

Table C6. Trends in the Rate of Return to Nonfinancial Corporate
Capital, 1950-77: Profits After Taxes (Straight Line Depreciation), Single Dummy

Equation	Constant Coefficient	Time	CEA	GAP STL	TR	UCAP FR	WM	D60	RHO	R̄2	DW	SEE
A.	-5.344 (-0.849)	-0.068 (-2.718)	0.110 (1.753)					2.721 (6.589)	0.143 (0.749)	0.782	1.786	0.790
B.	-15.559 (-1.989)	-0.073 (-3.479)		0.215 (2.716)				2.293 (5.273)	0.101 (0.527)	0.813	1.819	0.732
C.	-4.693 (-0.514)	-0.082 (-3.427)			0.102 (1.136)			2.969 (7.357)	0.143 (0.751)	0.766	1.812	0.818
D.	-1.026 (-0.307)	-0.078 (-3.665)				0.080 (2.014)		2.675 (6.668)	0.085 (0.444)	0.790	1.877	0.776
E.	-1.188 (0.443)	-0.096 (-4.323)					0.052 (1.684)	2.892 (7.570)	0.092 (0.482)	0.780	1.874	0.794

Note: Figures in parenthesis are "t" statistics. See table A for designation of variables.

Table C7. Trends in the Rate of Return to Nonfinancial Corporate
Capital, 1950-77: Profits After Taxes (NIPA) Plus Interest, Single Dummy

Equation	Constant Coefficient	Time	CEA	GAP STL	TR	UCAP FR	WM	D60	RHO	R̄²	DW	SEE
				INDEPENDENT VARIABLES					REGRESSION STATISTICS			
A.	-7.122 (-1.282)	0.026 (1.215)	0.128 (2.316)					2.575 (7.125)	0.105 (0.549)	0.777	1.794	0.712
B.	-16.028 (-2.278)	0.020 (1.076)		0.221 (3.094)				2.157 (5.566)	0.058 0.301	0.805	1.840	0.666
C.	-5.976 (-0.707)	0.011 (0.497)			0.115 (1.385)			2.823 (7.468)	0.155 (0.814)	0.747	1.795	0.758
D.	-1.246 (-0.405)	0.014 (0.720)				0.083 (2.274)		2.521 (6.823)	0.778 0.405	0.775	1.894	0.715
E.	0.697 (0.286)	-0.004 (-0.228)					-0.059 (2.081)	2.754 (8.014)	0.072 0.377	0.767	1.894	0.727

Note: Figures in parenthesis are "t" statistics. See table A for designation of variables.

Table C8. Trends in the Rate of Return to Nonfinancial Corporate
Capital, 1950-77: Profits Before Taxes (Straight Line Depreciation), Single Dummy

			INDEPENDENT VARIABLES							REGRESSION STATISTICS			
Equation	Constant Coefficient	Time	CEA	GAP STL	TR	UCAP FR	WM	D60		RHO	$\bar{R}^2$	DW	SEE
A.	-17.460 (-2.052)	-0.183 (-4.830)	0.306 (3.604)					2.654 (4.528)		0.300 (1.634)	0.866	1.784	0.993
B.	-34.806 (-3.798)	-0.207 (-7.859)		0.487 (5.244)				1.888 (3.612)		0.193 (1.020)	0.905	1.904	0.836
C.	-20.952 (-1.804)	-0.217 (-5.520)			0.337 (2.940)			3.246 (5.307)		0.326 (1.792)	0.847	1.804	1.062
D.	-3.143 (-0.753)	-0.217 (-1.294)				0.194 (3.944)		2.647 (4.973)		0.191 1.009	0.875	1.974	0.957
E.	1.148 (0.328)	-0.262 (-8.527)					0.141 (3.481)	3.161 (6.110)		0.178 (0.942)	0.863	1.917	1.004

Note: Figures in parenthesis are "t" statistics. See table A for designation of variables.

Table C9. Trends in the Rate of Return to Nonfinancial
Corporate Capital, 1955-77: With Perloff-Wachter GNP Gaps

Equation	Constant Coefficient	INDEPENDENT VARIABLES			REGRESSION STATISTICS			
		Time	GAP	D60	RHO	$\bar{R}^2$	DW	SEE
NIPINT	-19.624 (-2.527)	-0.115 (-3.330)	0.326 (4.111)	2.598 (5.221)	0.199 (0.955)	0.874	1.760	0.805
PATINT	+13.215 (-2.205)	-0.000 (-0.003)	0.193 (3.148)	2.328 (6.205)	0.089 (0.420)	0.833	1.805	0.654
ZBAD	-18.964 (-2.104)	-0.212 (-5.028)	0.320 (3.472)	2.692 (4.599)	0.255 (1.235)	0.883	1.744	0.917
PATJSL	-12.325 (-1.789)	-0.100 (-3.425)	0.185 (2.627)	2.418 (5.568)	0.131 (0.621)	0.841	1.798	0.739

Note: Figures in parenthesis are "t" statistics. See table A for designation of variables.

105

Table C10. Trends in the Rate of Return to Nonfinancial Corporate Capital, 1950-77: Profits Before Taxes (NIPA) Plus Interest, Varied Dummy

Equation	Constant Coefficient	Time	CEA	GAP STL	GAP Q	GAP TR	UCAP FR	UCAP WM	D60	D7075	RHO	$\bar{R}^2$	DW	SEE
A.	-19.232 (-2.727)	-0.057 (-1.635)	0.323 (4.608)						2.225 (4.415)	-1.164 (-1.481)	0.233 (1.246)	0.858	1.904	0.843
B.	-34.910 (-4.070)	-0.108 (-3.743)		0.489 (5.617)					1.635 (3.354)	-0.298 (-0.552)	0.202 (1.072)	0.884	1.935	0.761
C.	-2.991 (-0.771)	-0.106 (-3.114)					0.193 (4.207)		2.281 (4.350)	-0.631 (-1.014)	0.235 (1.255)	0.845	2.035	0.897
D.	0.570 (0.181)	-0.145 (-4.222)						0.148 (4.063)	2.707 (5.360)	-0.875 (-1.412)	0.201 (1.066)	0.839	1.988	0.898
E.	-21.018 (-2.008)	-0.094 (-2.222)				0.337 (3.264)			2.801 (4.748)	-1.062 (-1.524)	0.356 (1.978)	0.816	1.805	0.959
F.	-19.506 (-2.886)	-0.084 (-2.499)			0.323 (4.681)				2.377 (5.285)	-1.031 (-2.106)	0.121 (0.571)	0.899	6.844	0.725

Note: Figures in parenthesis are "t" statistics. See table A for designation of variables.

Table C11. Trends in the Rate of Return to Nonfinancial Corporate Capital
1950-77: Profits Before Taxes (Straight Line Depreciation)

	Constant	INDEPENDENT VARIABLES		GAP			UCAP				REGRESSION STATISTICS			
Equation	Coefficient	Time	CEA	STL	Q	TR	FR	WM	D60	D7075	RHO	$\bar{R}^2$	DW	SEE
A.	-17.687 (-2.381)	-0.137 (-3.726)	0.307 (4.157)						2.293 (4.324)	-1.590 (-2.565)	0.223 (1.190)	0.893	1.906	0.890
B.	-33.266 (-3.676)	-0.185 (-6.132)		0.472 (5.134)					1.715 (3.341)	-0.758 (-1.334)	0.186 (0.986)	0.912	1.936	0.800
C.	-2.629 (-0.654)	-0.185 (-5.424)					0.188 (3.958)		2.359 (4.433)	-1.065 (-1.681)	0.188 (0.996)	0.887	2.042	0.910
D.	1.098 (0.337)	-0.221 (-6.342)						0.141 (3.748)	2.772 (5.364)	-1.309 (-2.050)	0.166 (0.877)	0.881	1.985	0.930
E.	-20.634 (-1.903)	-0.173 (-4.154)				0.333 (3.112)			2.888 (4.871)	-1.463 (-2.066)	0.317 (1.736)	0.868	1.835	0.980
F.	-17.978 (-2.445)	-0.163 (-4.442)			0.308 (4.094)				2.419 (4.941)	-1.467 (-2.757)	0.134 (0.632)	0.915	1.866	0.780

Note: Figures in parenthesis are "t" statistics. See table A for designation of variables.

Table C12. Trends in the Rate of Return to Nonfinancial Corporate
Capital, 1950-77: Profits After Taxes (NIPA) Plus Interest

| | | | | INDEPENDENT VARIABLES | | | | | | | | REGRESSION STATISTICS | | | |
| | | | | GAP | | | UCAP | | | | | | | | |
Equation	Constant Coefficient	Time	CEA	STL	Q	TR	FR	WM	D60	D7075	RHO	$\bar{R}^2$	DW	SEE
A.	-8.333 (-1.490)	0.044 (1.616)	0.139 (2.505)						2.381 (6.002)	-0.554 (-1.170)	0.120 (0.629)	0.784	1.759	0.704
B.	-15.854 (-2.166)	0.022 (0.960)		0.218 (2.942)					2.122 (5.143)	-0.158 (-0.347)	0.078 (0.407)	0.799	1.808	0.680
C.	-1.166 (-0.370)	0.022 (0.863)					0.081 (2.180)		2.428 (5.981)	-0.311 (-0.641)	0.107 (0.560)	0.771	1.864	0.725
D.	0.538 (0.217)	0.007 (0.257)						0.060 (2.083)	2.611 (6.732)	-0.414 (-0.854)	0.104 (0.544)	0.767	1.863	0.731
E.	-6.374 (-0.754)	0.025 (0.879)				0.118 (1.422)			2.649 (6.276)	-0.499 (-0.955)	0.197 (1.043)	0.749	1.749	0.759
F.	-14.070 (-2.384)	0.012 (0.408)			0.201 (3.328)				2.193 (5.589)	-0.425 (-0.991)	0.082 (0.385)	0.839	1.796	0.646

Note: Figures in parenthesis are "t" statistics. See table A for designaton of variables.

108

Table C13. Trends in the Rate of Return to Nonfinancial Corporate Capital, 1950-77: Profits After Taxes (Straight Line Depreciation)

			INDEPENDENT VARIABLES								REGRESSION STATISTICS			
				GAP			UCAP							
Equation	Constant Coefficient	Time	CEA	STL	Q	TR	FR	WM	D60	D7075	RHO	$\bar{R}^2$	DW	SEE
A.	-6.668 (-1.131)	-0.036 (-1.240)	0.122 (2.082)						2.390 (5.710)	-0.975 (-1.959)	0.137 (0.721)	0.810	1.784	0.736
B.	-13.999 (-1.814)	-0.054 (-2.174)		0.199 (2.540)					2.140 (4.915)	-0.623 (-1.297)	0.104 (0.544)	0.823	1.817	0.710
C.	-0.648 (-0.200)	-0.549 (-2.110)					0.074 (1.939)		2.438 (5.859)	-0.753 (-1.515)	0.101 (0.525)	0.805	1.879	0.746
D.	1.091 (0.425)	-0.068 (-2.555)						0.053 (1.768)	2.600 (6.472)	-0.852 (-1.696)	0.108 (0.563)	0.800	1.874	0.755
E.	-5.683 (-0.658)	-0.052 (-1.826)				0.111 (1.304)			2.658 (6.275)	-0.909 (-1.723)	0.172 (0.906)	0.790	1.786	0.775
F.	-12.336 (-1.957)	-0.069 (-2.234)			0.183 (2.848)				2.196 (5.239)	-0.848 (-1.851)	0.086 (0.404)	0.861	1.842	0.689

Note: Figures in parenthesis are "t" statistics. See table A for designation of variables.

Table D1a. Rates of Return on Profits Before Tax (NIPA)
Plus Interest: Actual and Cyclically Adjusted*
(percent)

	Actual	CEA gap	St. Louis Fed gap	Perloff-Wachter gap	"Trend" gap
			Cyclically adjusted by:		
1949	13.1	15.0	16.5	n.a.	14.7
1950	15.5	15.7	16.2	n.a.	15.6
1951	15.1	13.9	14.9	n.a.	13.8
1952	13.1	12.1	13.2	n.a.	12.0
1953	12.3	11.4	12.0	n.a.	11.5
1954	11.5	12.5	13.4	n.a.	12.5
1955	14.4	14.2	14.6	14.2	13.9
1956	12.4	12.7	13.1	12.3	12.0
1957	11.2	12.2	12.5	11.6	10.9
1958	9.5	11.9	12.8	11.6	10.3
1959	12.1	13.5	13.7	12.8	11.7
1960	11.2	13.1	13.3	12.5	11.0
1961	11.0	13.2	13.6	12.8	11.3
1962	12.7	14.0	14.0	13.6	12.5
1963	13.6	14.9	14.3	14.2	13.6
1964	14.6	15.3	14.5	14.5	14.6
1965	15.9	15.9	14.6	14.7	15.9
1966	15.7	14.8	14.0	13.8	15.4
1967	13.8	13.3	12.8	12.7	14.0
1968	13.7	12.9	12.5	12.1	13.1
1969	11.9	11.5	11.8	10.5	11.2
1970	9.4	10.5	11.4	9.7	9.6
1971	9.7	11.1	11.8	10.3	9.8
1972	10.7	11.2	12.0	10.3	9.8
1973	10.3	10.1	10.9	9.1	8.5
1974	7.9	9.6	10.0	8.7	7.8
1975	8.3	11.9	12.3	11.0	9.9
1976	9.4	12.1	11.6	11.1	9.9
1977	9.6	11.8	10.6	10.4	9.4
Averages:					
1949-77	12.1	12.8	13.1	11.9**	11.9
1950-59	12.7	13.0	13.6	12.5**	12.4
1960-69	13.4	13.9	13.5	13.1	12.9
1949-69	13.1	13.5	13.7	12.9**	12.8
1970-77	9.4	11.0	11.3	10.1	9.4

*Denominator consists of stock of reproducible physical assets at replacement cost.
**Initial year average is 1955.

Table D1b. Rates of Return on Profits Before Tax (NIPA)
Plus Interest: Actual and Cyclically Adjusted*[1]
(percent)

		Cyclically adjusted by:			
		CEA	St. Louis	Perloff-Wachter	"Trend"
	Actual	gap[2]	Fed gap	gap	gap
1948	13.1	12.4	n.a.	n.a.	n.a.
1949	11.6	13.1	14.2	n.a.	12.8
1950	13.0	13.2	13.6	n.a.	13.0
1951	13.1	12.2	13.0	n.a.	12.1
1952	11.5	10.7	11.6	n.a.	10.7
1953	10.8	10.1	10.5	n.a.	10.2
1954	10.2	11.0	11.7	n.a.	11.0
1955	12.4	12.2	12.5	12.2	12.1
1956	10.5	10.7	11.1	10.4	10.2
1957	9.7	10.5	10.7	10.0	9.5
1958	8.5	10.4	11.1	10.1	9.1
1959	10.7	11.8	11.9	11.2	10.4
1960	9.9	11.4	11.5	10.9	9.7
1961	9.7	11.5	11.7	11.1	9.9
1962	11.2	12.3	12.2	11.9	11.0
1963	11.9	12.9	12.4	12.4	11.9
1964	12.7	13.3	12.6	12.6	12.7
1965	13.7	13.7	12.7	12.8	13.7
1966	13.4	12.7	12.0	12.0	13.2
1967	11.9	11.5	11.1	11.0	12.0
1968	11.7	11.0	10.7	10.4	11.3
1969	10.1	9.8	10.0	9.0	9.6
1970	8.1	9.0	9.7	8.3	8.3
1971	8.3	9.4	10.0	8.8	8.4
1972	9.1	9.5	10.1	8.8	8.5
1973	8.6	8.4	9.0	7.6	7.3
1974	6.4	7.8	8.0	7.0	6.4
1975	7.2	10.1	10.3	9.3	8.3
1976	8.1	10.2	9.8	9.4	8.5
1977	8.1	9.8	8.9	8.7	8.0

Table D1b. (continued)

Averages:					
1948-77	10.59	11.11	11.26[3]	10.27[4]	10.34[3]
1950-59	11.04	11.29	11.78	10.81[4]	10.83
1960-69	11.62	12.01	11.72	11.40	11.51
1948-69	11.42	11.72	11.82[3]	11.21[4]	11.25[3]
1970-77	7.89	9.29	9.49	8.51	7.95

[1] Cyclically adjusted by GNP gaps. See p. 60 for definition of gaps.
[2] Feldstein/Summers adjustment update.
[3] Initial year average is 1949.
[4] Initial year average is 1955.

Note: These rates differ from those in Table D1a because the denominator represents December 31 values to conform with the Feldstein/Summers procedures, as well as including land with other physical assets. Other tables in this report use a two year average of December 31 values in the denominator and exclude land.

Table D1c. Rates of Return on Profits Before Tax
(NIPA) Actual and Cyclically Adjusted*
(percent)

	Actual	CEA gap	St. Louis Fed gap	Cyclically adjusted by: Perloff-Wachter gap	"Trend" gap
1949	12.6	14.5	16.0	n.a.	14.3
1950	15.0	15.3	15.7	n.a.	15.1
1951	14.7	13.5	14.5	n.a.	13.3
1952	12.6	11.6	12.7	n.a.	11.5
1953	11.8	10.9	11.4	n.a.	11.0
1954	10.9	12.0	12.8	n.a.	12.0
1955	13.8	13.6	14.0	13.6	13.3
1956	11.8	12.1	12.5	11.7	11.4
1957	10.5	11.5	11.8	10.9	10.2
1958	8.7	11.1	12.0	10.8	9.5
1959	11.2	12.6	12.8	11.9	10.8
1960	10.3	12.2	12.4	11.6	10.1
1961	10.0	12.3	12.6	11.8	10.3
1962	11.6	13.0	12.9	12.5	11.4
1963	12.4	13.7	13.1	13.0	12.4
1964	13.4	14.2	13.3	13.3	13.4
1965	14.6	14.6	13.3	13.4	14.6
1966	14.3	13.4	12.6	12.4	14.0
1967	12.2	11.7	11.2	11.1	12.4
1968	12.0	11.2	10.8	10.4	11.4
1969	10.0	9.6	9.9	8.6	9.3
1970	7.1	8.3	9.1	7.4	7.4
1971	7.4	8.8	9.5	8.0	7.6
1972	8.4	8.9	9.7	8.0	7.5
1973	7.9	7.7	8.5	6.7	6.0
1974	5.2	7.0	7.3	6.0	5.1
1975	5.9	9.6	9.9	8.6	7.5
1976	7.2	9.9	9.4	8.9	7.7
1977	7.4	9.6	8.4	8.2	7.2
Averages:					
1949-77	10.7	11.5	11.7	10.4**	10.6
1950-58	12.1	12.4	13.0	11.8**	11.8
1960-69	12.1	12.6	12.2	11.8	11.5
1949-69	12.1	12.6	12.8	11.8**	11.8
1970-77	7.1	8.7	9.0	7.7	7.0

*Denominator consists of stock of reproducible physical assets at replacement cost.
**Initial year average in 1955.

D1d. Rates of Return on Profits After Tax (NIPA)
Plus Interest: Actual and Cyclically Adjusted*
(percent)

	Actual	CEA gap	St. Louis Fed gap	Perloff-Wachter gap	"Trend" gap
				Cyclically adjusted by:	
1949	8.0	8.8	9.5	n.a.	8.4
1950	6.9	7.0	7.2	n.a.	6.9
1951	5.8	5.3	5.7	n.a.	5.5
1952	5.7	5.3	5.8	n.a.	5.4
1953	5.0	4.6	4.8	n.a.	4.8
1954	5.6	6.0	6.4	n.a.	5.9
1955	7.1	7.0	7.2	7.0	7.0
1956	5.8	5.9	6.1	5.7	5.7
1957	5.4	5.8	6.0	5.6	5.3
1958	4.8	5.8	6.3	6.0	5.0
1959	6.2	6.8	6.9	6.6	6.1
1960	5.9	6.7	6.8	6.6	5.8
1961	5.8	6.7	6.9	6.8	5.9
1962	7.4	8.0	8.0	7.9	7.3
1963	7.9	8.4	8.2	8.2	7.9
1964	9.0	9.3	9.0	8.9	9.0
1965	9.9	9.9	9.3	9.2	9.9
1966	9.8	9.4	9.0	8.8	9.7
1967	8.8	8.6	8.4	8.2	8.8
1968	8.1	7.8	7.6	7.2	7.9
1969	6.9	6.7	6.8	6.1	6.7
1970	5.6	6.1	6.5	5.8	5.7
1971	5.9	6.5	6.8	6.2	5.9
1972	6.8	7.0	7.4	6.6	6.6
1973	6.2	6.1	6.4	5.5	5.7
1974	4.1	4.8	5.0	4.6	4.1
1975	5.2	6.7	7.0	6.7	5.6
1976	5.6	6.7	6.6	6.5	5.7
1977	5.8	6.7	6.2	6.3	5.8
Averages:					
1949-77	6.6	6.9	7.0	6.8**	6.6
1950-59	5.8	6.0	6.2	6.2**	5.8
1960-69	8.0	8.2	8.0	7.8	7.7
1949-69	6.9	7.1	7.2	7.3**	6.8
1970-77	5.6	6.3	6.5	6.0	5.6

*Denominator consists of stock of reproducible physical assets at replacement cost.
**Initial year average is 1955.

Table D1e. Rates of Return on Profits After Tax
(NIPA) Actual and Cyclically Adjusted*
(percent)

				Cyclically adjusted by:	
				Perloff-	
		CEA	St. Louis	Wachter	"Trend"
	Actual	gap	Fed gap	gap	gap
1949	7.5	8.3	9.1	n.a.	8.0
1950	6.5	6.6	6.8	n.a.	6.5
1951	5.5	5.0	5.4	n.a.	5.1
1952	5.2	4.8	5.3	n.a.	4.9
1953	4.5	4.1	4.4	n.a.	4.3
1954	5.0	5.4	5.9	n.a.	5.3
1955	6.5	6.4	6.6	6.3	6.3
1956	5.2	5.4	5.6	5.2	5.1
1957	4.8	5.2	5.4	5.0	4.7
1958	4.0	5.0	5.6	5.3	4.2
1959	5.4	6.0	6.1	5.8	5.2
1960	5.0	5.8	6.0	5.8	4.9
1961	4.8	5.8	6.0	5.9	4.9
1962	6.2	6.8	6.8	6.8	6.2
1963	6.7	7.3	7.1	7.1	6.7
1964	7.7	8.0	7.7	7.6	7.7
1965	8.6	8.5	8.0	7.8	8.6
1966	8.4	8.0	7.5	7.2	8.3
1967	7.2	7.0	6.7	6.5	7.3
1968	6.4	6.0	5.8	5.4	6.2
1969	5.0	4.8	4.9	4.2	4.8
1970	3.3	3.8	4.3	3.5	3.4
1971	3.6	4.2	4.7	4.0	3.7
1972	4.5	4.7	5.1	4.3	4.2
1973	3.8	3.7	4.1	3.0	3.2
1974	1.5	2.2	2.5	2.0	1.5
1975	2.8	4.4	4.7	4.5	3.3
1976	3.4	4.6	4.5	4.4	3.6
1977	3.6	4.5	4.0	4.1	3.5
Averages:					
1949-77	5.3	5.6	5.7	5.3**	5.2
1950-59	5.3	5.4	5.7	5.5**	5.2
1960-69	6.6	6.8	6.7	6.4	6.3
1949-69	6.0	6.2	6.3	6.1**	5.8
1970-77	3.3	4.0	4.2	3.7	3.3

*Denominator consists of stock of reproducible physical assets at replacement cost.
**Initial year average is 1955.

Table D2a. Shares of Profits Before Tax (NIPA) and Labor Compensation
of Gross Product, Nonfinancial Corporations*
(percent)

	Profits Plus Net Interest	Compensation Of Employees	Other**
1948	19.4	63.9	16.7
1949	18.0	63.9	18.1
1950	20.1	62.3	17.6
1951	19.8	63.2	17.0
1952	17.3	64.9	17.8
1953	16.0	66.0	18.0
1954	15.7	65.9	18.4
1955	18.4	63.9	17.7
1956	16.3	65.4	18.3
1957	15.4	65.7	18.9
1958	13.9	66.0	20.1
1959	16.1	64.6	19.3
1960	14.7	65.3	20.0
1961	14.5	65.1	20.4
1962	15.9	64.2	19.9
1963	16.6	63.7	19.7
1964	17.3	63.3	19.4
1965	18.4	62.8	18.8
1966	18.2	63.5	18.3
1967	16.8	64.4	18.8
1968	16.5	64.5	19.0
1969	14.7	66.0	19.3
1970	12.2	67.3	20.5
1971	12.7	66.3	21.0
1972	13.6	66.1	20.3
1973	13.2	67.0	19.8
1974	11.0	68.4	20.6
1975	12.3	66.0	21.7
1976	13.4	65.8	20.8
1977	13.4	66.4	20.2
1978	13.1	62.2	19.7
Averages:			
1948-78	15.6	65.1	19.2
1950-59	16.9	64.8	18.3
1960-69	16.4	64.3	19.4
1948-69	16.7	64.5	17.9
1970-78	12.8	66.7	20.5

*Detail may not add to total due to rounding.
**Capital Consumption Allowance with capital consumption adjustment plus indirect taxes, plus transfers less subsidies.

Table D2b. Nonfinancial Corporations:
Contribution of Unit Factor Costs to
Changes in the Price Deflator
(percent)

	Implicit Price Deflator	Unit Nonlabor Cost	Unit Labor Cost	Unit Profits
1949	1.5	1.7	1.0	-1.2
1950	1.2	-.5	-.8	2.5
1951	5.2	.5	4.1	.6
1952	2.6	1.4	3.4	-2.2
1953	.8	.3	1.7	-1.2
1954	1.3	.8	.7	-.2
1955	1.6	-.4	-1.0	3.0
1956	3.9	1.1	4.1	-1.3
1957	3.2	1.6	2.4	-.8
1958	2.2	1.8	1.8	-1.4
1959	1.5	-.5	-.4	2.4
1960	1.0	.9	1.4	-1.3
1961	.3	.6	.0	-.3
1962	.3	-.4	-.6	1.3
1963	.0	-.1	-.6	.7
1964	1.0	-.2	.3	.9
1965	.9	-.2	.0	1.1
1966	1.9	-.1	2.0	.0
1967	2.7	1.2	2.7	-1.2
1968	3.3	1.0	2.2	.1
1969	4.1	1.6	4.2	-1.7
1970	4.6	3.4	4.4	-3.2
1971	4.3	1.5	1.8	1.0
1972	2.8	.0	1.6	1.2
1973	4.4	.8	3.8	-.2
1974	11.5	4.0	9.3	-1.8
1975	10.4	3.6	4.5	2.3
1976	5.4	.1	3.3	2.0
1977	5.9	.7	4.5	.7
1978	6.8	1.0	5.4	.4
Averages:				
1949-77	3.2	.9	2.2	.1
1950-59	2.4	.6	1.6	.1
1960-69	1.6	.4	1.2	.0
1970-77	6.2	1.7	4.3	.3
1973-77	7.4	1.7	5.1	.6

Note: Detail may not add to totals due to rounding.

Table D3. Effective Tax Rates, Nonfinancial Corporations

	Profits Before Tax (NIPA)	Taxes Paid	Profits After Tax (NIPA)	Effective Tax Rate	Maximum Tax Rate*
	Bil. Dol.				
1948	25.8	11.8	14.0	45.7	38.0
1949	23.0	9.3	13.7	40.4	38.0
1950	29.6	16.9	12.7	57.1	42.0
1951	33.4	21.2	12.2	63.5	50.8
1952	30.3	17.8	12.5	58.7	52.0
1953	29.9	18.5	11.4	61.9	52.0
1954	28.6	15.6	13.0	54.5	52.0
1955	38.2	20.2	18.0	52.9	52.0
1956	36.1	20.1	16.0	55.7	52.0
1957	35.0	19.1	15.9	54.6	52.0
1958	30.1	16.2	13.9	53.8	52.0
1959	39.7	20.7	19.0	52.1	52.0
1960	37.4	19.2	18.2	51.3	52.0
1961	37.4	19.5	17.9	52.1	52.0
1962	44.9	20.6	24.3	45.9	52.0
1963	50.0	22.8	27.2	45.6	52.0
1964	56.7	24.0	32.7	42.3	50.0
1965	66.1	27.2	38.9	41.1	48.0
1966	71.2	29.5	41.7	41.4	48.0
1967	67.2	27.7	39.5	41.2	48.0
1968	72.1	33.6	38.5	46.6	52.8
1969	66.4	33.3	33.1	50.2	52.8
1970	51.6	27.3	24.3	52.9	49.2
1971	58.7	29.9	28.8	50.9	48.6
1972	72.0	33.5	38.5	46.5	48.0
1973	76.0	39.6	36.4	52.1	48.0
1974	59.5	42.7	16.8	71.8	48.0
1975	76.9	40.6	36.3	52.8	48.0
1976	101.3	53.0	48.3	52.3	48.0
1977	113.9	59.0	54.9	51.8	48.0
1978	125.1	68.6	56.5	54.8	48.0
Averages:					
1948-78	58.9	27.7	26.6	51.4	47.7
1950-59	33.1	18.6	14.5	56.5	50.9
1960-69	57.0	25.7	31.2	45.8	50.8
1970-78	81.7	43.8	37.9	54.0	48.1

*Tax rate applicable to large corporations, where income generally exceeds $25,000.

Table D4a. Rates of Return, Nonfinancial Corporations*
Return on Reproducible Assets
(percent)

	Corporate Profits Before Taxes With IVA & CCADJ (NIPA)	Corporate Profits After Taxes With IVA & CCADJ**	Corporate Profits Before Taxes With IVA & CCADJ (NIPA)	Corporate Profits After Taxes With IVA & CCADJ**
	(With Interest)		(Without Interest)	
1947	13.9	6.6	13.4	6.1
1948	15.4	8.6	14.9	8.1
1949	13.1	8.0	12.6	7.5
1950	15.5	6.9	15.0	6.5
1951	15.1	5.8	14.7	5.4
1952	13.1	5.7	12.6	5.2
1953	12.3	5.0	11.8	4.5
1954	11.5	5.6	10.9	5.0
1955	14.4	7.1	13.8	6.5
1956	12.4	5.8	11.8	5.2
1957	11.2	5.4	10.5	4.8
1958	9.5	4.8	8.7	4.0
1959	12.1	6.2	11.2	5.4
1960	11.2	5.9	10.3	5.0
1961	11.0	5.8	10.0	4.8
1962	12.7	7.4	11.6	6.2
1963	13.6	7.9	12.4	6.7
1964	14.6	9.0	13.4	7.7
1965	15.9	9.9	14.6	8.6
1966	15.7	9.8	14.3	8.4
1967	13.8	8.8	12.2	7.2
1968	13.7	8.1	12.0	6.4
1969	11.9	6.9	10.0	5.0
1970	9.4	5.6	7.1	3.3
1971	9.7	5.9	7.4	3.6
1972	10.7	6.8	8.4	4.5
1973	10.3	6.2	7.9	3.8
1974	7.9	4.1	5.2	1.5
1975	8.3	5.2	5.9	2.8
1976	9.4	5.6	7.2	3.4
1977	9.6	5.8	7.4	3.6
1978	9.5	5.5	7.3	3.3

Table D4a. (continued)

Averages:				
1948-78	12.1	6.6	10.7	5.3
1950-59	12.7	5.8	12.1	5.3
1960-69	13.4	8.0	12.1	6.6
1948-69	13.2	7.0	12.2	6.1
1970-78	9.4	5.6	7.1	3.3

*Designated profit measure as percent of stock of reproducible physical assets at replacement cost.
**Straight Line Depreciation.

Table D4b. Rates of Return Nonfinancial Corporations: Before Tax Return on Total Assets

	Profits Before Tax (NIPA)	Net Interest	Capital Income (1) + (2)	Total Assets*	Rates of Return	
					With Interest (3) ÷ (4)	Without Interest (1) ÷ (4)
	(1)	(2)	(3)	(4)	(5)	(6)
		(Bil. of Dol.)			(Percent)	
1948	25.8	.9	26.7	299.7	8.9	8.6
1949	23.0	1.0	24.0	308.0	7.8	7.5
1950	29.6	.9	30.5	351.4	8.7	8.4
1951	33.4	1.1	34.5	388.0	8.9	8.6
1952	30.3	1.2	31.5	407.6	7.7	7.4
1953	29.9	1.3	31.2	423.6	7.4	7.1
1954	28.6	1.6	30.2	438.7	6.9	6.5
1955	38.2	1.6	39.8	484.6	8.2	7.9
1956	36.1	1.7	37.8	528.1	7.2	6.8
1957	35.0	2.2	37.2	557.0	6.7	6.3
1958	30.1	2.7	32.8	578.6	5.7	5.2
1959	39.7	3.1	42.8	613.1	7.0	6.5
1960	37.4	3.5	40.9	631.1	6.5	5.9
1961	37.4	3.9	41.3	657.0	6.3	5.7
1962	44.9	4.5	49.3	689.1	7.2	6.5
1963	50.0	4.8	54.8	721.2	7.6	6.9
1964	56.7	5.3	62.0	761.9	8.1	7.4
1965	66.1	6.1	72.2	825.3	8.7	8.0
1966	71.2	7.4	78.6	894.9	8.8	8.0
1967	67.2	8.7	75.9	964.3	7.9	7.0

Table D4b. (continued)

	Profits Before Tax (NIPA)	Net Interest	Capital Income (1) + (2)	Total Assets*	Rates of Return	
					With Interest (3) ÷ (4)	Without Interest (1) ÷ (4)
		(Bil. of Dol.)			(Percent)	
	(1)	(2)	(3)	(4)	(5)	(6)
1968	72.1	10.1	82.2	1050.5	7.8	6.9
1969	66.4	13.1	79.5	1158.5	6.9	5.7
1970	51.6	17.0	68.6	1241.2	5.5	4.2
1971	58.7	17.9	76.6	1331.8	5.8	4.4
1972	72.0	19.1	91.1	1464.4	6.2	4.9
1973	76.0	23.1	99.1	1692.2	5.9	4.5
1974	59.5	29.9	89.4	1910.4	4.7	3.1
1975	76.9	30.8	107.7	2069.1	5.2	3.7
1976	101.3	30.7	132.0	2255.6	5.9	4.5
1977	113.9	33.7	147.6	2475.6	6.0	4.6
1978	125.1	37.2	162.3	2775.4	5.8	4.5
Averages:						
1948-77	54.3	10.5	64.8	978.3	7.3	6.2
1950-59	33.1	1.7	34.8	477.1	7.4	7.1
1960-69	56.9	6.7	63.6	835.4	7.6	6.8
1948-69	43.1	3.9	47.0	624.2	7.6	7.0
1970-78	81.7	26.6	108.3	1912.9	5.7	4.3

*Tangible assets at current cost, financial assets at book value.

Table D4c. Rates of Return Nonfinancial Corporations: After Tax Return on Total Assets:

	Profits Before Tax (NIPA)	Net Interest	Capital Income (1) + (2)	Total Assets*	Rates of Return	
					With Interest (3) ÷ (4)	Without Interest (1) ÷ (4)
	(1)	(2)	(3)	(4)	(5)	(6)
	(Bil. of Dol.)				(Percent)	
1948	14.0	.9	14.9	299.7	5.0	4.7
1949	13.7	1.0	14.7	308.0	4.8	4.4
1950	12.8	.9	13.7	351.4	3.9	3.6
1951	12.2	1.1	13.3	388.0	3.4	3.1
1952	12.6	1.2	13.8	407.6	3.4	3.1
1953	11.4	1.3	12.7	423.6	3.0	2.7
1954	13.0	1.6	14.6	438.7	3.3	3.0
1955	18.0	1.6	19.6	484.6	4.0	3.7
1956	16.0	1.7	17.7	528.1	3.4	3.0
1957	15.8	2.2	18.0	557.0	3.2	2.8
1958	13.8	2.7	16.5	578.6	2.9	2.4
1959	19.0	3.1	22.1	613.1	3.6	3.1
1960	18.3	3.5	21.8	631.0	3.5	2.9
1961	18.0	3.9	21.9	657.0	3.3	2.7
1962	24.2	4.5	28.7	689.1	4.2	3.5
1963	27.2	4.8	32.0	721.2	4.4	3.8
1964	32.7	5.3	38.0	761.9	5.0	4.3
1965	38.9	6.1	45.0	825.3	5.4	4.7
1966	41.7	7.4	49.1	894.9	5.5	4.7
1967	39.6	8.7	48.3	964.3	5.0	4.1
1968	38.5	10.1	48.6	1050.5	4.6	3.7

Table D4c. (continued)

	Profits Before Tax (NIPA)	Net Interest	Capital Income (1) + (2)	Total Assets*	Rates of Return (Percent)	
					With Interest (3) ÷ (4)	Without Interest (1) ÷ (4)
	(1)	(Bil. of Dol.) (2)	(3)	(4)	(5)	(6)
1969	33.2	13.1	46.3	1158.5	4.0	2.9
1970	24.3	17.0	41.3	1291.2	3.3	2.0
1971	28.8	17.9	46.7	1331.8	3.5	2.2
1972	38.5	19.1	57.6	1464.4	3.9	2.6
1973	36.4	23.1	59.5	1692.2	3.5	2.2
1974	16.8	29.9	46.7	1910.4	2.4	.9
1975	36.3	30.8	67.1	2069.1	3.2	1.8
1976	48.3	30.7	79.0	2255.6	3.5	2.1
1977	54.9	33.7	88.6	2475.6	3.6	2.2
1978	56.5	37.2	93.7	2775.4	3.3	2.0
Averages:						
1948-78	26.6	10.5	37.6	998.3	3.8	3.1
1950-59	14.5	1.7	16.2	477.1	3.4	3.1
1960-69	31.2	6.7	38.0	835.4	4.5	3.7
1948-69	22.0	3.9	26.0	624.2	4.0	3.5
1970-78	37.9	26.6	64.5	1912.9	3.4	2.0

*Tangible assets at current cost, financial assets at book value.

124

Table D5. Retained Earnings, Reported and Adjusted for IVA and
Replacement Cost of Depreciation for Nonfinancial Corporation
(Billion Dollars)

	Reported	Straight Line Depreciation	Double Declining Balance Depreciation
1948	13.5	7.4	6.5
1949	9.1	7.2	6.2
1950	13.6	4.8	3.8
1951	10.1	4.5	3.4
1952	8.1	4.8	3.8
1953	8.4	3.4	2.2
1954	8.2	4.8	3.6
1955	12.4	8.7	7.6
1956	11.6	6.0	4.4
1957	10.3	5.4	3.6
1958	7.3	3.6	1.9
1959	11.5	8.2	6.7
1960	8.7	6.8	5.4
1961	8.0	6.3	5.0
1962	10.3	11.5	10.2
1963	11.4	13.2	11.8
1964	15.4	17.4	15.8
1965	20.0	21.7	19.6
1966	21.9	23.6	20.7
1967	18.8	20.7	17.1
1968	17.6	17.8	13.8
1969	14.4	12.5	8.0
1970	8.0	4.4	-0.3
1971	13.3	8.8	4.2
1972	20.7	16.8	12.4
1973	29.2	12.5	7.5
1974	34.2	-9.2	-15.3
1975	32.2	7.9	1.6
1976	43.7	14.9	9.8
1977	45.5	16.0	10.5
1978	53.5	11.5	5.2
Averages:			
1948-78	17.76	9.8	7.0
1950-59	10.15	5.4	4.1
1960-69	14.65	15.2	12.7
1948-69	12.30	10.0	8.2
1970-78	31.14	9.3	4.0

Table D6. Profits After Tax (NIPA) as a Percent of
Depreciable Assets and of Stockholders'
Equity, Nonfinancial Corporations

	Depreciable Assets	Stockholders' Equity
1948	8.1	7.1
1949	7.5	6.6
1950	6.5	5.6
1951	5.5	4.9
1952	5.2	4.8
1953	4.5	4.2
1954	5.0	4.6
1955	6.5	5.8
1956	5.2	4.7
1957	4.8	4.4
1958	4.0	3.8
1959	5.4	4.9
1960	5.0	4.6
1961	4.8	4.4
1962	6.2	5.8
1963	6.7	6.4
1964	7.7	7.3
1965	8.6	8.2
1966	8.4	8.2
1967	7.2	7.2
1968	6.4	6.6
1969	5.0	5.2
1970	3.3	3.6
1971	3.6	4.0
1972	4.5	4.9
1973	3.8	4.0
1974	1.5	1.6
1975	2.8	3.0
1976	3.4	3.7
1977	3.6	3.8
1978	3.3	3.5
Averages:		
1948-78	5.3	5.1
1950-59	5.3	4.8
1960-69	6.6	6.4
1970-78	3.3	3.6

Note: Depreciable assets at replacement cost; annual estimates are averages of year-end figures. Equity revalues all physical assets at replacement cost.

Source: Department of Commerce and Federal Reserve Board.

Table D7. Capital Income, Profits (NIPA), and Reported Profits
Before Tax as a Percentage of Nonfinancial Gross
Corporate Product (1948-1977)

Year	Capital Income*	Profits (NIPA)**	Reported Profits
1948	19.4	18.8	23.2
1949	18.0	17.2	18.7
1950	20.1	19.5	25.3
1951	19.8	19.1	22.4
1952	17.3	16.6	18.5
1953	16.0	15.3	17.9
1954	15.7	14.9	16.7
1955	18.4	17.6	19.4
1956	16.3	15.6	18.0
1957	15.4	14.4	16.4
1958	13.9	12.7	14.3
1959	16.1	14.9	16.2
1960	14.7	13.5	14.2
1961	14.5	13.1	13.8
1962	15.9	14.4	14.1
1963	16.6	15.1	14.6
1964	17.3	15.9	15.3
1965	18.4	16.9	16.4
1966	18.2	16.5	16.1
1967	16.8	14.8	14.4
1968	16.5	14.5	14.4
1969	14.7	12.3	12.6
1970	12.2	9.2	9.8
1971	12.7	9.7	10.5
1972	13.6	10.7	11.3
1973	13.2	10.1	12.3
1974	11.1	7.4	12.7
1975	12.3	8.8	11.6
1976	13.4	10.2	13.2
1977	13.4	10.3	13.0
1978	13.1	10.1	13.5

Averages:			
1948-78	15.6	13.9	15.5
1950-59	16.9	16.1	18.5
1960-69	16.4	14.7	14.6
1948-69	16.66	15.5	16.7
1970-78	12.8	9.6	12.0

*Profits (NIPA) plus Interest.
**Reported profits with IVA plus Capital Consumption Adjustment.

Table D8. Alternative Measures of Gap
Between Actual and Potential and Trend GNP
(percent)

	CEA gap*	St. Louis Fed gap	Perloff-Wachter gap	"Trend" gap
1949	95.4	94.2	n.a.	95.8
1950	99.4	-98.8	n.a.	99.8
1951	102.8	100.3	n.a.	103.4
1952	102.3	99.7	n.a.	102.8
1953	102.2	100.6	n.a.	102.1
1954	97.4	96.7	n.a.	97.3
1955	100.5	99.7	100.6	101.2
1956	99.2	98.7	100.2	101.1
1957	97.7	97.8	99.0	100.8
1958	94.2	94.3	95.3	98.0
1959	96.5	97.3	98.4	101.1
1960	95.4	96.4	97.2	100.5
1961	94.6	95.6	96.0	99.2
1962	96.7	97.8	98.1	100.6
1963	96.9	98.8	98.6	100.0
1964	98.2	100.1	100.3	99.9
1965	100.1	102.7	102.7	99.9
1966	102.1	102.9	104.1	100.8
1967	101.1	101.7	102.5	99.5
1968	101.9	102.1	103.6	101.5
1969	101.0	100.2	103.0	101.8
1970	97.2	96.5	99.3	99.3
1971	96.7	96.4	98.6	99.6
1972	98.7	97.8	100.9	102.3
1973	100.6	99.6	102.7	104.7
1974	95.8	96.5	98.2	100.1
1975	91.3	93.2	93.9	95.9
1976	93.5	96.2	96.2	98.6
1977	94.7	98.3	98.1	100.4

*January 1978 Economic Report of the President.

Table D9. After-Tax Capital Income, Profits (NIPA), and Reported
Profits as a Percentage of Nonfinancial Gross
Corporate Product (1948-1977)

Year	Capital Income*	Profits (NIPA)**	Reported Profits
1948	10.9	10.2	14.6
1949	11.0	10.3	11.7
1950	9.0	8.4	14.2
1951	7.6	7.0	10.3
1952	7.5	6.9	8.8
1953	6.5	5.8	8.4
1954	7.6	6.8	8.5
1955	9.0	8.3	10.1
1956	7.6	7.0	9.4
1957	7.5	6.6	8.5
1958	7.0	5.9	7.4
1959	8.3	7.2	8.4
1960	7.8	6.6	7.3
1961	7.7	6.3	6.9
1962	9.3	7.8	7.4
1963	9.7	8.2	7.7
1964	10.6	9.1	8.6
1965	11.5	9.9	9.5
1967	10.6	8.7	8.3
1968	9.8	7.7	7.7
1969	8.5	6.1	6.5
1970	7.4	4.3	5.0
1971	7.8	4.8	5.5
1972	8.6	5.7	6.3
1973	7.9	4.8	7.1
1974	5.8	2.1	7.4
1975	7.7	4.2	6.9
1976	8.0	4.9	7.8
1977	8.0	5.0	7.7
1978	7.6	4.6	7.9
Averages:			
1948-78	8.6	6.8	8.4
1950-59	7.8	7.0	9.4
1960-69	9.7	8.0	7.9
1948-69	8.8	7.6	8.8
1970-78	7.64	4.5	6.8

*Profits (NIPA) after-tax plus Interest paid.
**Profits after-tax with IVA plus Capital Consumption Adjustments.

Table D10. Trends in Rates of Return on Capital Income, with Various "GAP" Measures* (Nonfinancial Corporations)

		Time	UCAP FR	UCAP WM	CEA gap	St. Louis Fed gap	"Trend" gap	Perloff-Wachter	See	P
A.	F/S 1949-76	-0.14 (1.56)							1.20	0.70
	Revised F/S 1949-77	-0.16 (1.78)							1.16	0.71
	Update 1950-77	-0.13 (1.30)							1.16	0.72
B.	F/S 1949-76	-0.13 (1.62)	0.17 (4.25)						0.92	0.72
	Revised F/S 1949-77	-0.12 (1.71)	0.16 (4.00)						0.94	0.70
	Update 1950-77	-0.11 (1.38)	0.16 (4.00)						0.96	0.69
C.	F/S 1949-76	-0.18 (1.80)		0.14 (4.67)					0.96	0.77
	Revised F/S 1949-77	-0.17 (1.89)		0.13 (3.25)					0.98	0.75
	Update 1950-77	-0.15 (1.50)		0.12 3.00					1.00	0.75

Table D10. (continued)

D.	Time	UCAP FR	UCAP WM	CEA gap	St. Louis Fed gap	"Trend" gap	Perloff-Wachter	See	P
F/S 1949-76	-0.07 (0.88)			0.34 (4.86)				0.89	0.75
Revised F/S 1949-77	-0.07 (0.88)			0.33 (4.12)				0.90	0.74
Update 1950-77	-0.06 (0.75)			0.33 (4.12)				0.91	0.73
Alternative A 1950-77	-0.11 (2.20)				0.46 (5.75)			0.79	0.58
Alternative B 1950-1977	-0.11 (0.92)					0.28 (3.10)		1.00	0.79
Alternative C 1950-77	-0.14 (1.17)						0.35 (3.95)	0.89	0.75

*Rates of return represent profits before tax (NIPA) plus interest paid in numerator and replacement value of fixed capital inventories and land at end-year values in the denominator.

Table D11. Comparison of Coefficients for Time After
Allowance for Indicated Pressure Variable

	Time Alone	CEA	GAPS STL	Q	UCAP FR	WM
			Pressure Variable			
Profits After Tax						
—Straight line	-0.087	-0.045	-0.068	-0.074	-0.102	-0.141
	(-0.759)	(-0.431)	(-0.927)	(-0.748)	(0.899)	(-1.166)
—Double Declining	-0.079	-0.039	-0.063	-0.068	-0.093	-0.125
Balance	(-0.718)	(-0.374)	(-0.868)	(-0.704)	(-0.843)	(-0.992)
Profits Before Tax						
—Straight Line	-0.213	-0.123	0.188	-0.189	-0.244	-0.223
	(-1.771)	(1.186)	(-3.561)	(-2.183)	(-2.101)	(-1.560)
—Double Declining	-0.211	-0.119	-0.188	-0.188	-0.240	-0.209
Balance	(-1.807)	(-1.124)	(-3.435)	(-2.203)	(-2.071)	(-1.401)
Profits After Tax Plus Interest						
—Straight Line	0.207	0.046	0.024	-0.019	-0.007	0.245
	(0.060)	(2.493)	(0.350)	(-0.199)	(-0.064)	(-0.382)
—Double Declining	0.013	2.523	0.028	0.024	-0.001	-0.033
Balance	(0.121)	(0.555)	(0.423)	(0.269)	(-0.011)	(-0.274)
Profits Before Tax Plus Interest						
—Straight Line	-0.198	-0.034	-0.097	-0.696	-0.149	-0.128
	(-1.033)	(-0.377)	(-2.159)	(-1.222)	(-1.372)	(-0.988)
—Double Declining	-0.118	-0.031	-0.098	-0.097	-0.147	-0.115
Balance	(-1.053)	(-0.335)	(-2.084)	(-1.239)	(-1.384)	(-0.852)

Table D12. A Compendium of Rates of Return to Nonfinancial Corporations in the Recent Literature

| | Profits plus Interest as percentage of Tangible Capital | | Percentage of Net Worth, After Tax | | | | "q": Ratio of market value of corporations to replacement cost | | | |
| | Before Tax | After Tax | | | | | Equity plus Debt / Tangible Capital | | | Equity / Net Worth |
	Feldstein & Summers	Holland & Myers	CEA	Malkiel & von Furstenburg	Kopcke	Cagan & Lipsey	CEA	Ciccolo	Holland & Myers	Cagan & Lipsey
1955	12.4	11.0	6.5	—	—	11.4	.93	1.40	.86	.94
1956	10.6	8.3	5.8	—	—	13.0	.92	.95	.89	.89
1957	9.8	5.4	4.9	4.8	—	6.3	.86	.83	.82	.75
1958	8.5	4.3	3.8	3.9	—	4.4	.87	1.06	.79	.99
1959	10.7	5.7	4.9	5.0	—|	7.2	1.05	1.20	1.01	1.00
1960	9.9	4.7	4.4	4.6	—	4.8	1.02	1.14	.97	.98
1961	9.8	4.9	4.3	4.3	—	3.3	1.15	1.44	1.13	1.19
1962	11.2	6.4	5.6	5.9	—	5.9	1.09	1.26	1.09	1.02
1963	11.9	6.7	6.1	6.2	—	7.7	1.20	1.46	1.22	1.14
1964	12.8	8.6	7.1	7.4	—	8.6	1.29	1.58	1.28	1.20
1965	13.7	10.6	8.1	7.9	17	11.5	1.36	1.68	1.37	1.26
1966	13.4	10.5	8.8	8.5	18	14.4	1.20	1.22	1.23	1.05
1967	11.9	8.8	7.7	7.4	19	12.0	1.21	1.36	1.22	1.20
1968	11.7	7.7	7.0	7.1	14	10.6	1.26	1.47	1.19	1.31
1969	10.2	6.1	6.3	5.8	22	14.4	1.13	1.21	1.13	1.04

Table D12. (continued)

| | Profits plus Interest as percentage of Tangible Capital | | Percentage of Net Worth, After Tax | | | | "q": Ratio of market value of corporations to replacement cost | | | |
| | Before Tax | After Tax | | | | | Equity plus Debt Tangible Capital | | | Equity Net Worth |
	Feldstein & Summers	Holland & Myers	CEA	Malkiel & von Furstenburg	Kopcke	Cagan & Lipsey	CEA	Ciccolo	Holland & Myers	Cagan & Lipsey
1970	8.1	5.2	5.0	4.4	11	4.3	.91	1.00	.84	.99
1971	8.4	6.5	4.5	4.8	11	4.0	1.01	1.15	.98	1.10
1972	9.2	7.8	6.2	5.5	13	9.0	1.09	1.25	1.04	1.16
1973	8.6	7.9	5.8	5.4	18	16.7	1.03	1.10	1.02	.76
1974	6.4	4.4	9.9	3.6	18	16.0	.76	.73	.94	.42
1975	6.9	6.1	6.1	4.9	12	4.8	.75	.87	.73	.52
1976	7.9	3.5	5.8	5.1	—	.6	.84	1.03	—	.62
1977	—	—	5.9	—	—	9.2	.79	.91	—	.50

Source: Adapted from Cagan and Lipsey (1978), pp. 74-75.

Table D13. Nonfinancial Corporations:
Relation of Debt to Equity

	Credit Market Instruments	Stockholder's Equity (Net Worth) (Bil. of Dol.)	Credit Market Instruments As Percent of Stockholder's Equity (1) ÷ (2)
	(1)	(2)	(3)
1948	62.8	121.0	51.9
1949	64.6	130.8	49.4
1950	71.3	143.7	49.6
1951	79.6	159.2	50.0
1952	86.8	170.5	50.8
1953	91.0	183.2	49.7
1954	98.8	193.4	49.5
1955	104.2	208.3	50.0
1956	114.8	224.3	51.2
1957	124.7	238.5	52.3
1958	133.2	249.5	53.4
1959	143.5	265.5	54.0
1960	154.1	274.3	56.2
1961	164.3	287.3	57.2
1962	176.3	303.2	58.1
1963	189.1	317.9	59.5
1964	202.5	337.0	60.1
1965	223.0	359.1	62.1
1966	247.2	389.0	64.4
1967	274.1	409.2	67.0
1968	305.9	429.9	71.0
1969	340.4	460.2	74.0
1970	375.3	478.8	78.4
1971	408.3	508.7	80.3
1972	455.4	541.3	89.1
1973	519.9	589.7	88.9
1974	597.8	648.7	92.1
1975	626.4	709.9	88.3
1976	673.6	775.2	86.9
1977	749.7	828.9	90.4
1978	834.2	902.2	92.5
Averages:			
1948-78	280.3	381.8	65.3
1950-59	104.5	203.6	51.1
1960-69	227.6	356.2	63.0
1970-77	582.3	664.2	86.9

Note: Detail may not add to totals due to rounding.
Source: Based on Flow of Funds, Federal Reserve.

Bibliography

Aaron, Henry J. Inflation and the Income Tax. The Brookings Institution, 1976.

American Accounting Association, "Accounting for Land, Buildings and Equipment," The Accounting Review 39 (July 1964), pp. 695-97.

Boshan, Charlotte, and Walter Ebank. "A New Method of Measuring Economic Growth Fluctuations." 1978 Proceedings: American Statistical Association, Business and Economic Section.

Boskin, Michael. "Taxation Saving, and the Rate of Interest." Journal of Political Economy (April 1978), pp. 571-589.

Cagan, Phillip and Robert Lipsey. The Financial Effects of Inflation. National Bureau of Economic Research, 1978.

Chimerine, L. and S. Hunmelstein. "Corporate Profits in the United States," Business Economics (Jan. 1979), pp. 78-82.

Ciccolo, J. Four Essays on Monetary Policy. Unpublished Ph.D. dissertation, Yale University, 1975.

Clark, Peter K. "Capital Formation and the Recent Productivity Slowdown," paper presented at Annual Meeting, American Economic Association, 1977 (mimeo).

Corcoran, Patrick J. "Inflation, Taxes, and Corporate Investment Incentives." Federal Reserve Bank of New York Quarterly Review (Autumn 1977), pp. 1-10.

The Council of Economic Advisors. The 1977 Economic Report of the President. 1977.

The Council of Economic Advisors. The 1978 Economic Report of the President. 1978.

The Council of Economic Advisors. The 1979 Economic Report of the President. 1979.

Denison, Edward F. Accounting for United States Economic Growth 1929-1969. The Brookings Institution, 1974.

Ehrbar, A.F. "Those Pension Plans are Even Weaker Than You Think." Fortune (November 1977), pp. 104-14.

Eisner, R. "Investment and the Frustration of Econometricians" American Economic Review, May 1969.

Feldstein, Martin S. "Does the United States Save Too Little?" American Economic Review (February 1977), pp. 116-21.
_____. "The Welfare Cost of Capital Income Taxation." Journal of Political Economy (April 1978).
_____. "Private Pensions and National Savings." Journal of Public Economics (forthcoming).
Feldstein, Martin, and Lawrence Summers. "Is the Rate of Profit Falling?" Brookings Papers on Economic Activity, 1 (1977), pp. 211-29.
Fellner, William. "Comments and Discussion." Brookings Papers on Economic Activity, 1 (1976): 58.
Freeman, R.B. "Investment in Human Capital and Knowledge." Capital for Productivity and Jobs, Ed: Shapiro, Eli and W. White, Englewood Cliffs, N.J.: Prentice Hall, 1977, pp. 96-123.
Greenspan, Allan. "Investment Risk: The New Dimension of Policy." The Economist (August 6, 1977), pp. 31-35.
Hall, Robert E. "Investment, Interest Rates, and the Effects of Stabilization Policies." Brookings Papers on Economic Activity, 1 (1977): 61-103.
Holland, Daniel M., and Stewart C. Myers. Trends in Corporate Profitability and Capital Costs. Cambridge: Sloan School of Management, Massachusetts Institute of Technology, 1977.
Kopcke, Richard. "Trends in the Rate of Corporate Profit." New England Economic Review, Federal Reserve Bank of Boston (May-June 1978), pp. 36-60.
_____. "Are Stocks a Bargain." New England Review, Federal Reserve Bank of Boston (May-June 1979).
Malkiel, Burton G. "Reports of the Death of Common Stock are Greatly Exaggerated." Fortune (November 1977), pp. 156-162.
Malkiel, Burton G., and George M. von Furstenberg. "Financial Analysis in an Inflationary Environment." Journal of Finance (May 1977), pp. 575-88.
McCracken, Paul, et al. Towards Full Employment and Price Stability. O.E.C.D., 1977.
Musgrave, John C. "Fixed Non-Residential Business and Residential Capital in the U.S., 1925-1975." Survey of Current Business, Office of Economic Analysis, U.S. Department of Commerce, 1976 and updated.
Nordhaus, William D. "The Falling Share of Profits." Brookings Papers on Economic Activity, 1 (1974): 169-217.
Okun, Arthur M., and George L. Perry. "Notes and Numbers on the Profits Squeeze." Brookings Papers on Economic Activity, 1970, pp. 466-73.
Perloff, Jeffery M., and Michael L. Wachter. A Production Function-Nonaccelerating Inflation Approach to Potential Output: Is Measured Potential Output Too High? Philadelphia: University of Pennsylvania Press, 1978.
Rasche, Robert H., and John A. Tatom. "Potential Output and Its Growth Rate," U.S. Productive Capacity: Estimating the Utilization Gap. St. Louis: Washington University Center for the Study of American Business, 1977.

Runyan, Herbert. The Profits Controversy Revisited. Unpublished. Federal Reserve Bank of San Francisco, 1978.

Sandilands, F.E.P. Inflation Accounting. Report of the Inflation Accounting Committee. London: Her Majesty's Stationery Office, 1975.

Schultze, Charles L. "Falling Profits, Rising Profit Margins, and the Full-Employment Profit Rate." Brookings Papers on Economic Activity, 2 (1975): 449-471.

Shoven, John B., and Jeremy I. Bulow. "Inflation Accounting and Nonfinancial Corporate Profits: Financial Assets and Liabilities." Brookings Papers on Economic Activity, 1 (1976): 15-66.

_____. "Inflation Accounting and Nonfinancial Corporate Profits: Physical Assets." Brookings Papers on Economic Activity, 3 (1975): 557-661.

Stekler, H.O. Profitability and Size of Firm. Berkeley: Institute of Business and Economic Research, University of California, 1963.

Terborgh, George. Realistic Depreciation Policy. MAPI, 1954.

_____. "Inflation and Profits." Financial Analysts Journal (May-June 1974), pp. 19-23.

_____. Inflation and Profits. Machinery and Allied Products Institute, 1976.

Tideman, T. Nicholas, and D. Tucker, "The Tax Treatment of Business Profits under Inflationary Conditions. Inflation and the Income Tax. Ed. H. Aaron. Brookings Institution. 1976, pp. 33-80.

Tobin, James. "A General Equilibrium Approach to Monetary Theory." Journal of Money, Credit and Banking (February 1969), pp. 15-29.

U.S. Department of Commerce. "National Income, 1954 Edition." Survey of Current Business, 1954.

U.S. Department of Commerce. Survey of Current Business, March 1976 and updated.

Index

Aaron, Henry J., 27
Accounting convention vs. Economic concepts, 25-27
and accrual accounting, 51
and inflation accounting, 5, 27-30
Allocation of resources. See Economic policies

Bond yields. See Interest rates and Cost of capital
Book profits. See Accounting conventions and Historical cost

Cagan, Phillip, and Robert Lipsey, 25, 27, 49-51, 59
Capacity to produce and employment, 23
Capacity utilization
Commerce Department rate of, 70
long-term "natural rate" of, 40
normal productivity at full rate of, 46
Wharton rate of, 62, 70
Capital consumption adjustment, 28
and early use by Nordhaus, 37-38
effect on profit of, 36
and 1976 NIPA revision, 27

Capital consumption adj. (cont'd)
and real value of debt, 36
and replacement costs, 32, 71
Capital consumption allowance, 27-29, 71-72, 74-75
Capital formation
and economic policy, 22
and market forces, 23, 24
and productivity growth, 22
and "social return" on capital investment, 40
and sufficiency of investment, 46-47, 69-70, 83
Capital Income, 11, 32, 37
as percent of GNP, 6
decline since 1968 of, 37-38
effective tax rate on, 43
pre- vs. posttax concepts of, 4, 36
weight of interest component of, 11
See also Profitability: Various measures; and Rates of return: Various measures
Capital-labor ratio
and the effects of its low growth in the 1970s, 22, 83
Capital-output ratio
and its effect on profit shares, 10, 37
Capital stock, 11-12
See also Capital formation

About the Author

HERMAN I. LIEBLING (Ph.D. – American University, Washington, D.C.) is presently the Frank Lee and Edna Smith Professor of Economics and Business at Lafayette College and Consultant to the Department of the Treasury. Prior to September 1976, he was senior economic advisor to several Secretaries of the Treasury with responsibilities related to the nature of the general domestic economic and financial outlook and technical assistance on formation of overall macroeconomic policy. Dr. Liebling also served as the Treasury's career service delegate on the Federal interagency "Troika," the group concerned with macroeconomic policies in the Federal Government, and, during 1969-76, was the Treasury's chief forecaster of the domestic economy.

For these activities, Dr. Liebling received the Meritorious Service Award of the Treasury Department in 1969. In 1973 he was nominated by the Department for the Rockefeller Public Service Award, and in 1976 received the Department's Exceptional Service Award.

Pergamon Policy Studies